Stitches:
New Approaches

Stitches:
New Approaches

Jan Beaney

Photographs by Dudley Moss

B.T. Batsford Limited   London

First published 1985

© Jan Beaney 1985

All rights reserved. No part of this publication
may be reproduced in any form or by any means
without permission from the Publishers

ISBN 0 7134 4272 7

Designed by Robert and Jean Wheeler

Photoset by Servis Filmsetting Ltd, Manchester

Printed in Great Britain by
R. J. Acford Ltd, Chichester, Sussex
for the Publishers

B.T. Batsford Ltd,
4 Fitzhardinge Street,
London W1H oAH

Contents

Acknowledgments

I would like to express my sincere thanks to the following people for their help, encouragement and friendship during the preparation of this book: Julia Caprara, Rosemary Ewles, Jean Jennings, Eirian Short, Denys Short, Margaret Suckling, Ann Sutton, Audrey Walker, Pam Watts, Members of the 62 Group, Members of the Practical Study Group, The Somerset Branch of the Embroiderers' Guild, and Carolyn Walker for typing the script.

My very special thanks to Jane Clarke and Jean Littlejohn, to all the Embroidery students from Windsor and Maidenhead College, to Dudley Moss for his superb photographs and to Steve, Nick and Victoria for being so understanding and supportive at all times.

My appreciation and thanks go to J & P Coats Limited for allowing me to use some of the stitch diagrams from *100 Embroidery Stitches* and to the Embroiderers' Guild for permitting me to photograph examples from the historical collection.

Note
All drawings and embroideries are by the author unless otherwise credited.

Foreword

The aim of this book is to encourage people to enjoy stitches and stitching and to explore the endless range of effects and textures that these can give. Once a stitch has been mastered and worked in the conventional way, some liberties can be taken. Using some guidelines initially, unusual surfaces can be created.

This book is not intended as a dictionary of stitches and will not attempt to cover every stitch. There are excellent books on the market offering a comprehensive list. Although many stitch 'families' have been included, the main intention is to give the reader the choice of going past the 'correct' and conventional method of working and spacing a particular stitch by suggesting starting points for new approaches.

Each stitch is first presented in the traditional or predictable way of working; this is followed by suggestions for spacing and working it by less usual and experimental methods using a variety of yarns. Many stitches are also shown being used in creative, interpretative ways. Stitches worked with even spacing and size can be very beautiful and perfectly suited to certain embroidery projects. However, freer, interpretative stitchery can also build up rich textural surfaces offering their own characteristics which can be most useful for the creative embroiderer.

Stitchery:
A personal view

At school I disliked stitchery and needlework so fervently that I would do anything to avoid the lessons. In those days pupils queued up to see the needlework mistress and with cunning I would drop my work several times and each time on retrieving it, reposition myself near the end of the line. Of course this resulted in limited stitching time. The experience of working long, endless rows of the same-sized stitch in one type of thread, unpicking and reworking them, lingers long in the mind. These pieces of work took for ever to finish and looked very tired and grubby on completion. Some pieces were made into handkerchief sachets – a present for mother!

My lack of enthusiasm for this pastime was, I am sure, due to my experience in infant school when I was expected to work a large Union Jack flag in solid chain stitch. (Incidentally, my despair over that stitch has only been rectified whilst working pieces for this book.)

After about the third year at secondary school, stitchery did not feature in my life until I attended art school. In my final year, I had the good fortune to join Eirian Short's embroidery class and she made me aware of the endless possibilities that stitchery and other embroidery techniques offer.

In most instances I like stitches to give me a textural experience. Initially on looking at a piece of work, I react with a basic 'gut' feeling to the impact of the subject, composition, the quality of the surface or originality of the colour scheme. This applies equally to any type of work whether it is an abstract piece, stylized or an interpretation of an observed surface. With few exceptions, the recognition of the stitches used comes after the joy of being excited by the surface in general.

I am continually thrilled by the extensive range of stitched surfaces, from thick, darned and woven areas to delicate lacy threadwork. The effect of strong, spiky, dynamic stitches can indicate movement or disquiet whereas chunky, chiselled, sculptured blocks of stitchery can suggest solidity or stability. By contrast, areas of straight stitches worked in identical fine

Interpretation of 'Thrift and Daisies' worked in cretan stitch. Areas of colour were painted with dye before the stitches were worked.

threads but placed in varying directions offer subtle changes of tone.

I prefer stitchwork to be uncomplicated; this sometimes means working with only one or two stitches and their varying arrangements. At times this sought-after simplicity can be achieved by overstitching to such an extent that an interesting, rich surface results which has a unified feel, a wholeness. I often react quite strongly against embroideries which include so many stitches that the design becomes a general 'hotchpotch' – over-busy areas all vying for pride of place or position.

In general, I enjoy the experience of choosing and handling varied yarns followed by the satisfaction of stitching through fabric and building up interesting patterns and surfaces.

Dried bullrushes (peeled). The cylinders are stitched with cotton and raffia using herringbone stitch. (*Geraldine Ormonde*.)

Stitches for functional embroidery

Many readers who love to look at and to embellish functional embroidery with traditional stitches worked in an orthodox way may be dismayed by the general exclusion of this approach in the following pages. However, a few guidelines seem appropriate.

Functional embroidery needs to be carefully considered and stitches, threads and fabrics chosen most thoughtfully. Examination jargon comes to mind: suitability for purpose, durability, washability and wearability. Thread, fabric and stitch decoration should be suitable for the intended purpose of the article or garment. It should be decided whether the finished piece is to be washed or dry-cleaned. A general rule is to match cotton thread to cotton fabric, silk to silk and synthetic to synthetic.

Stitches should be carefully selected so as not to lose their characteristics by continual washing, wearing and ironing. Generally, loose stitches are not suitable. More flamboyant, unusual surfaces can be created for garments or articles intended for limited use or special occasions.

Many good books cover this area of working most adequately, offering hints, recommendations and ways of working. This book concentrates on the reader who wishes to experiment freely with stitches. By breaking the so-called rules and developing the stitch to its limits, new surfaces can be achieved. The enjoyment of these experiences will, I hope, broaden the reader's expressionistic and interpretative approach to stitchery.

Starting points:
1 Choice of background fabrics

As a general rule, the fabric chosen should be firm enough to hold the weight of the stitchery without puckering or pulling out of shape. The more dense the area of stitchery desired, the stronger or firmer the material should be. In most instances a plain-coloured fabric should be chosen as boldly patterned, woven or printed ones can distract from the stitches if this fact has not been considered adequately at the outset. Just one fine, brightly coloured thread woven into the material could easily dominate the final effect.

For fine, delicate stitchery, a closely woven or smooth fabric is usually the most suitable. Transparent fabrics present exciting challenges and can give unique effects but care should be taken to consider whether the thread passing from stitch to stitch at the back of the work, which might be visible from the front, is acceptable. If a finer fabric is chosen and a highly textured area is required to be worked on it, stitches should be selected which are not worked continually through the fabric; couching and composite stitches could be considered.

Fabrics which have been woven with a slubbed or looped yarn are attractive and give an interesting surface but they can be infuriating if fine, even stitches are required as the weave will often dictate the placing of the needle. However, this need not be a problem if a more haphazard stitch arrangement is wanted. Heavily ridged fabric, such as repp, is often too tough to stitch through comfortably. Fabrics with a pile, such as velvet, tend to limit the choice of stitches used.

Loosely woven fabrics offer another starting point and some composite stitches using horizontal or vertical bars as a base can be worked directly onto the warp or weft threads. However, some of the fabrics possessing these suitable qualities may need to be backed by a firm, finer fabric to support the stitchery.

Many people prefer to work with fabrics made from natural fibres rather than synthetic ones but this is a matter of personal choice, cost and availability. Stitches should be tried out on a

variety of materials as it is always interesting to see how the stitch is affected by the ground fabric.

Suitable fabrics include:

> hessian (burlap), linen scrim, Aida
> calico (unbleached cotton)
> flannel
> furnishing – curtain – upholstery
> some dress-weight fabrics

Coarse scrim, sacking and net vegetable bags have a limited use, but superb effects can often be obtained from using unusual background materials, even though they present some working difficulties and have their limitations.

Background fabrics:
Top row Hessian (burlap) – coarsely woven silk
2nd row Heavyweight calico – upholstery fabric
3rd row Lightweight calico – linen scrim
4th row Rayon curtain fabric – coarsely woven cotton fabric.

Starting points:
2 Threads

It is generally recommended when embarking on an embroidery project that the threads selected should be able to be pulled easily through the chosen ground fabric. This is good advice to follow when working stitchery for a functional item or garment. It is essential that the stitches lie flat and do not cobble the surface and affect the hang or drape of a dress or the required flatness of a traycloth.

For purely decorative work, this rule may sometimes be discarded; it is possible to use a stiletto to pierce the fabric to enable a thicker and more textured thread to be pulled through. Some threads that appear too large for a certain material can be eased through by using a larger needle. However, if a thread is so thickness and lustre and can be single, twisted or multi-stranded. combination of fabric and thread is not suitable.

Free stitchery may also have a less ordered arrangement on the back of the work than conventional stitching, causing a slightly puckered top surface. This can be removed by damp-stretching on completion of the picture or panel.

There is a very wide range of threads available to the embroiderer today. Some threads are manufactured specifically for hand and machine embroidery and include yarns made from wool, linen, cotton, silk and synthetic fibres. They vary in thickness and lustre and can be single, twisted or multi-stranded. Often more readily available in local shops are knitting and crochet yarns which are made in varying plys. Some are slubbed, looped or have a short pile finish. Others are glossy, smooth, hairy, wiry, shaded, multi-coloured or incorporate metallic or lustre fibres.

Textured weaving yarns, carpet thrums, sewing cottons, metal threads, cord, tape and ribbons offer a further choice. Some of these items can be purchased for reasonable prices in markets. They can be bought in white or natural colours, then dyed to the desired hue.

Threads can be withdrawn from fabric, vegetable bags or sacks. A variety of string, raffia, twine and other lacings can be

Threads specifically made for embroidery:
Top row From left to right: soft embroidery cotton, linen, matgarn, crewel wool, stranded cotton, coton perlé.
Bottom row Tapestry wool, reels of metallic and machine cotton, synthetic metallicized thread, coton à broder and coton perlé.

17

found in stationers, household stores, chandlers or garden centres.

Yarns can be made by cutting long strips of leather, suede, fabric, nylon tights or plastic sheeting. These can be worked to make interesting surfaces if used on a suitable ground material.

It is worthwhile collecting all types of threads and experimenting with them on a range of backgrounds, discovering the limitations of working particular yarns.

Some of the novelty or heavily textured threads will not adapt well and can break if pulled continually through ground fabric. However, they can look most effective used on top of a basic stitch already worked in another thread or they can be couched directly in place.

Threads, including a wide range of slubbed and looped weaving, knitting and crochet yarns, tape and ribbon.

Starting points:
3 Needles

If you make a collection of needles, stitch experiments need not be inhibited. Choosing the right needle for the thread and fabric will make the stitching much easier and more enjoyable. The following types of needles come in varying sizes:

Beading: long and very fine – for sewing beads and sequins

Between: a short, fine needle used for quilting and general sewing

Sharp: a fine needle for general purpose sewing

Chenille: short with a large eye – suitable for stitching with coarser yarns

Crewel: smaller than the chenille and useful for many embroidery projects

Tapestry: a needle with a blunt point – useful for canvas work, counted thread embroidery and stitches which are built up one on top of another.

Heavy embroidery needles, short pile rug or knitter's needles are ideal for use with very thick threads. Large-eyed, flexible, plastic bodkins can be purchased from haberdashery departments or crafts suppliers.

Needles. From top to bottom: beading, betweens, sharps, chenille, crewel, tapestry heavy embroidery, knitter's, plastic bodkin, disposable spatula (from a motorway service station – not strong but useful for simple lacing and threading through). Right-hand side: a fid, obtainable from a ship's chandler – useful for thick yarns on very loosely woven fabric.

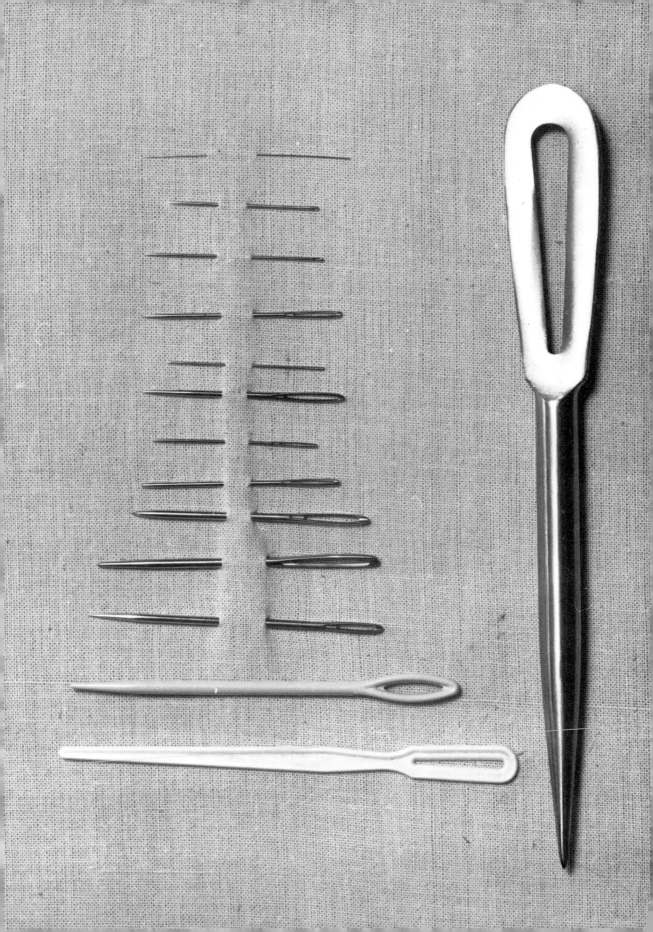

Starting points:
4 Frames

Embroidery frames are usually available from department stores or specialist shops, many of which provide a mail order service.

Round or tambour frames (ring, hoop) are adequate for smaller pieces of embroidery. If working with delicate fabrics, binding the rings of the frame with tape or bandage will help to eliminate frame marks on the material. Tissue paper can also be inserted to protect the cloth.

Rectangular frames are more useful for larger works. These include:

1. plain wooden frames made quite easily at home
2. old wooden picture frames – from jumble sales etc.
3. canvas stretchers – available from artists' materials suppliers
4. slate frames – available from shops specializing in embroidery equipment

Material to be stretched over the first three types of frame can be held in place by staples. A large staple gun or tacker would be more suitable than a small stapler manufactured for office use. Drawing pins (thumb tacks) can also be used but it is sometimes advisable to cover them with masking tape to prevent the thread looping around the pins during stitching. Care should be taken to ensure that the grain of the cloth is straight and lying at right angles to the sides of the frame. The material should be stapled or pinned at the centre first and then outwards to the corners. The fabric should be tightly stretched over the frame on completion.

Slate frames are often thought of as the proper or traditional embroidery frames. They require much careful thought and preparation at the outset. Frames fitted with wooden screws have the advantage that the tautness of the cloth can be adjusted during the work process. Many general books on embroidery techniques describe fully this method of framing up.

Some stitches such as couching, straight stitches or seeding, are best worked with the fabric stretched taut on the frame. However, other stitches, such as cretan, fly and spanish knotted feather are best worked in the hand, even though the fabric usually needs to be damp-stretched on completion.

The use of frames is a matter of trial and error, experience and individual choice.

An approach to stitchery

The following quotations seem relevant to the aims of this book.

Without stitches there could be no art of embroidery. They are the means by which fanciful ideas and memories of pleasant things can be figured upon fabrics.

A stitch should be chosen for use because it expresses perfectly the subject to be embroidered. . . .

Stitches, apart from what they express, possess qualities such as beauty of form, ingenuity and mystery, for they are sometimes curiously wrought, and in this there is charm. As a rule not enough is made of texture in embroidered work. By the aid of stitches a monotonous surface can be transformed at will into a richly varied one. The technique of the needle is so naive and delightful that it can afford to be daring.

Mrs Archibald Christie,
Samplers & Stitches, 1920

Let us sometimes be playful, although we need not be frivolous.
Rebecca Crompton, *Modern Design in Embroidery*, 1936

The person concerned only with the busy-time aspect of the craft, interested only in making things for the sake of doing and of the things themselves rather than in the personal gratification of completing a unique conception, ends up with satisfaction based only upon the skill of the craft and of the relief of the completion of the work. . . . The crafts, therefore, must enhance rather than destroy their purpose of life. If the activity were to include the more personal involvement of conceiving, planning and designing, as well as executing, the total experience would be richer and more rewarding, the individualism or the personality of the practitioner more part of the work.
Nik Krevitsky, *Stitchery: Art and Craft*, 1966

As in all things, ideas and certain approaches have been suggested before, years or maybe decades ago. These quotations from the past are still relevant and some of the sentiments are echoed in this book. The only difference is that today one's experience has broadened, other creative avenues have been explored and new and interesting materials are now available. The same problems and observations are being tackled on a different level and with new starting points. As with fashion design, basic concepts can be repeated but at each re-emergence of a particular shape, subtle changes made by the designer's individual treatment and choice of cut, fabric and decoration, offer something new and original to consider.

It is hoped that the format and selected starting points in this book offer a different approach and emphasis.

It is accepted that it can be very pleasurable just to stitch for the sake of stitchery but sadly, at school many students were taught, and are still being taught, embroidery stitches in a dull and monotonous way. As already stated, rows of beautifully executed, evenly spaced stitches can be most appropriate and absolutely right for some projects but other avenues can be explored, resulting in further inventive, interpretative and tactile surfaces.

Therefore the purpose of this book is to suggest ways of exploring the possibilities of creating beautiful and sometimes unusual and original surfaces from one or a limited number of stitches. It is not intended to give any answers – just the starting points so that individual, visual interpretations can be built up. This will help in the interpretation of observed pattern or texture in the appropriate colour, thread and scale, creating the desired surface.

The following sections suggest how to explore a stitch in detail. To illustrate this approach, two stitches have been worked showing variations of the initial starting points or thought processes. The same stitches worked by other people will result in further effects because individual workers will always choose to exaggerate different features, selecting other threads, fabrics and a different scale of working.

By selecting a stitch, possibly one that initially appears unsuitable, and working through the starting points suggested on the following pages, a whole work project could begin. Not surprisingly, some stitches will develop during these experiments into other known stitches, but more often, new, intriguing patterns and shapes will result.

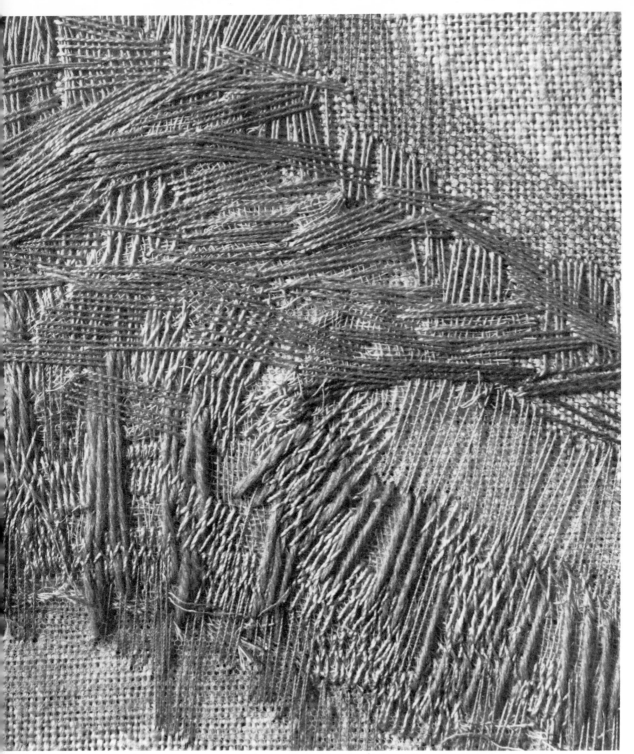

Detail from 'Autumn Landscape', showing straight and cretan stitches.

Exploring two stitches

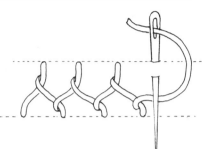

CRETAN STITCH

Cretan-stitch 'feathers' decorating a griffin. Detail from a seventeenth-century crewel work hanging. Crewel wools on linen/cotton twill. British (*Embroiderers' Guild Collection*.)

Stitches worked in a conventional way. Notice the effects achieved by varying the amount of fabric taken up within each stitch.

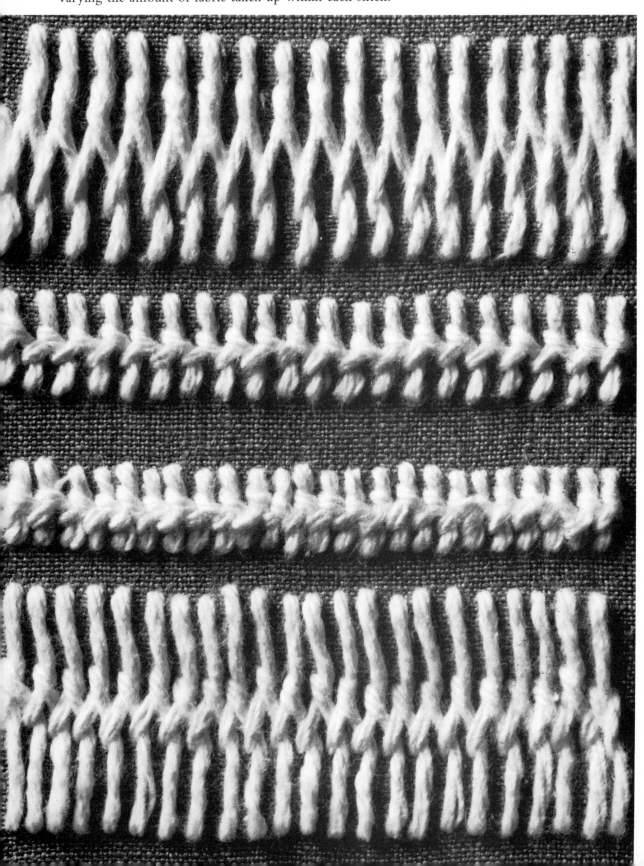

○ Work the stitch in a variety of threads: matt, smooth, fine, twisted, thick, hairy, slubbed etc.

○ Cut fabrics into strips and use instead of yarn. Try
   ribbons, braids, tape or other trimmings.

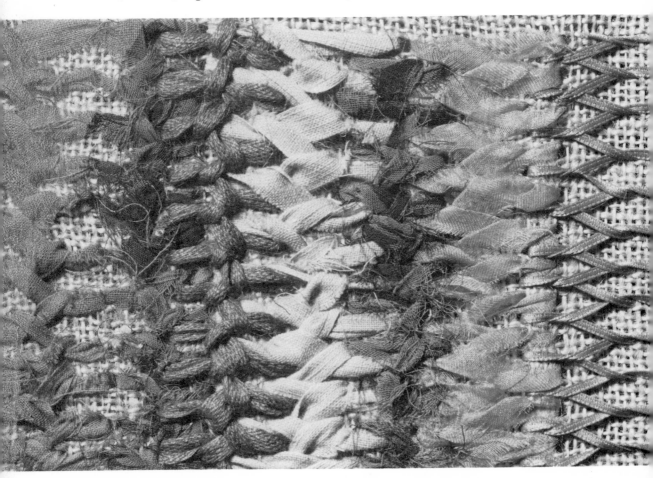

○ Vary the size of the stitch. Work as large as the thread, stitch and ground fabric will allow. Work the stitch as small as possible using a fine thread.

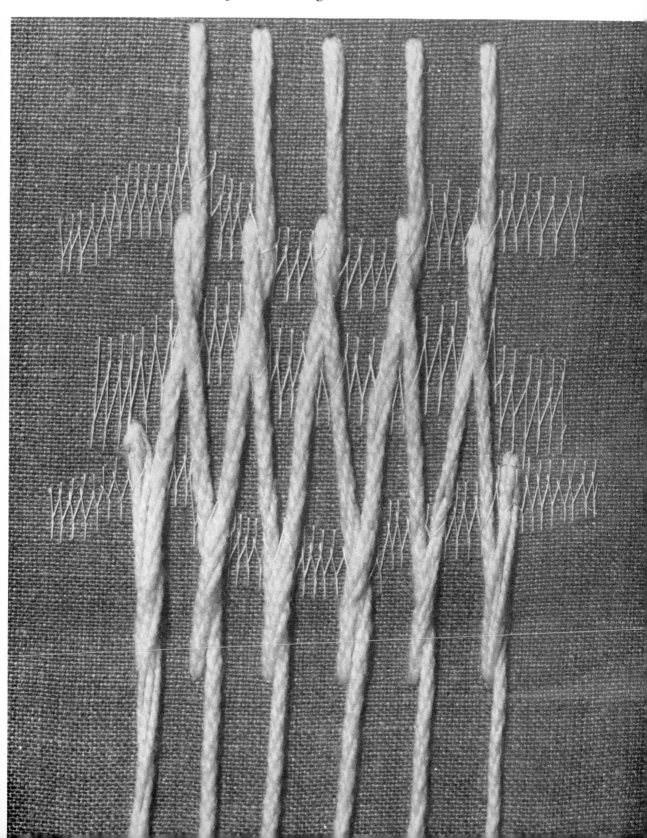

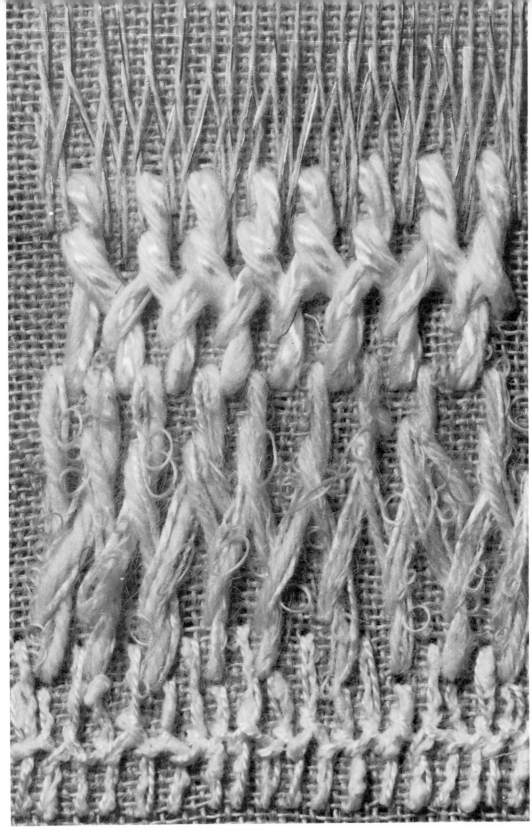

○ Use several different threads in one needle.

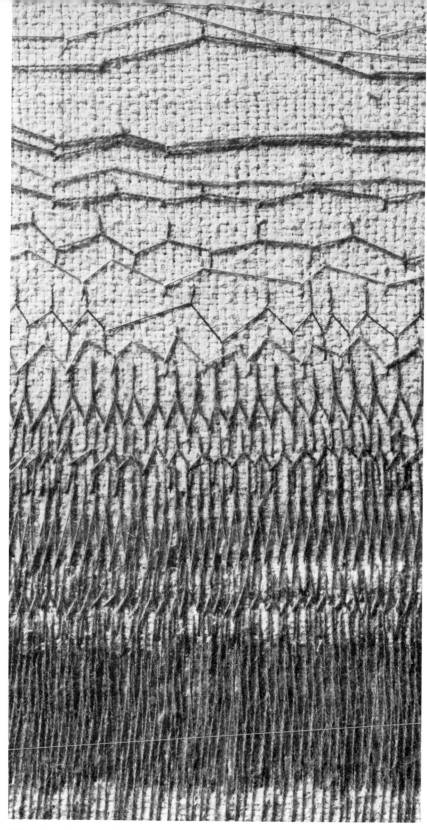

○ Work the stitches very closely: tightly packed together.

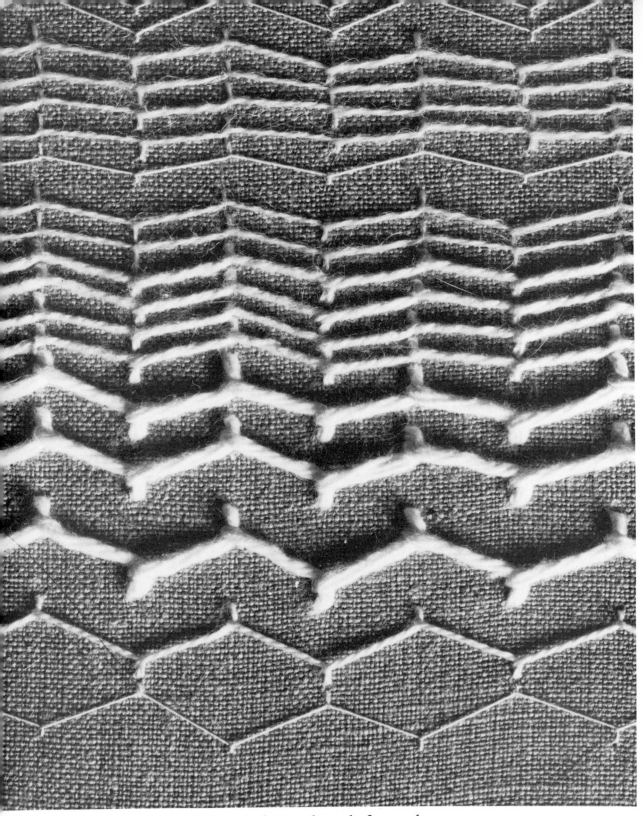

○ Now try working the stitch in a broad, fat or short manner.

○ Try working the stitch closely together and far apart, varying the spacing within one line of stitchery.

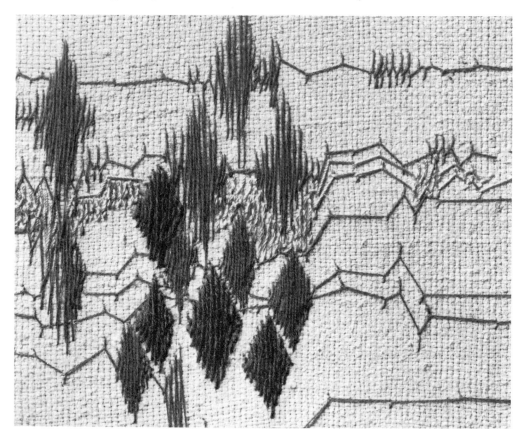

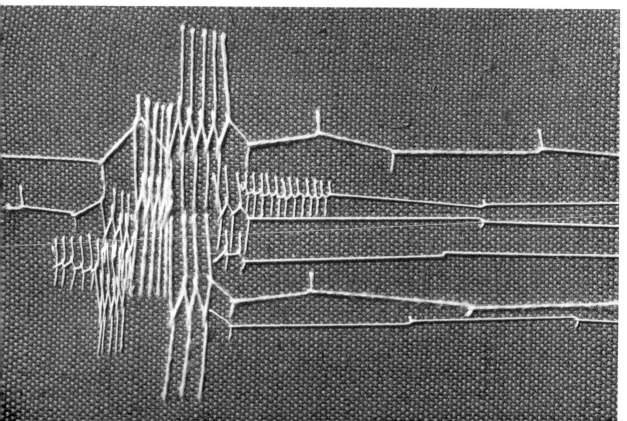

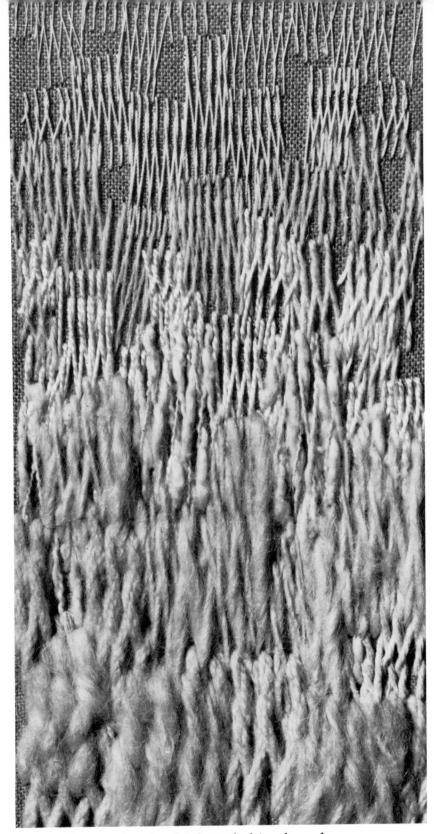

○ Work the stitches in thick and thin threads.

○ Experiment with coloured yarns. Vary the tone within one colour scheme. Work stitches in primary or complementary colours.

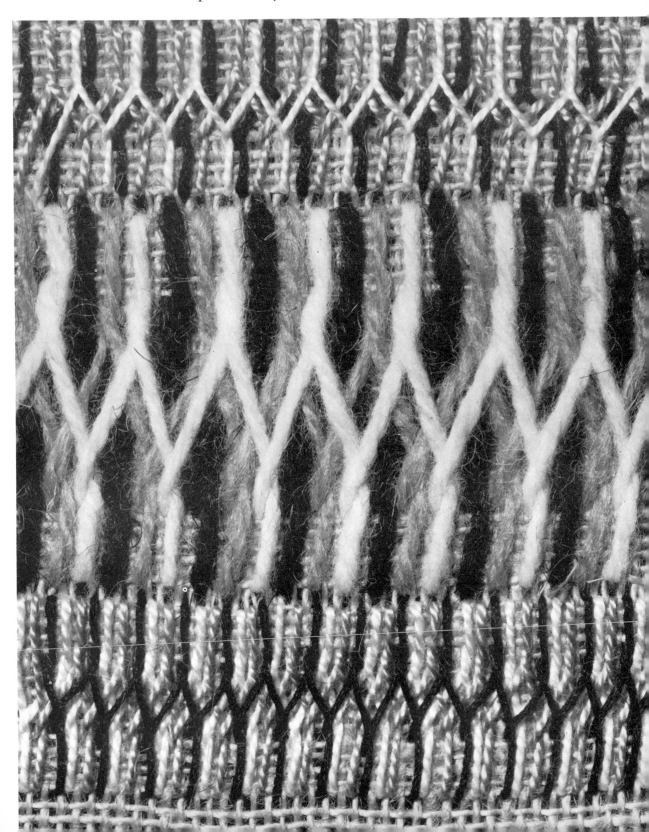

○ If possible work the stitch in a one-sided manner,
partially formed or with an uneven emphasis.

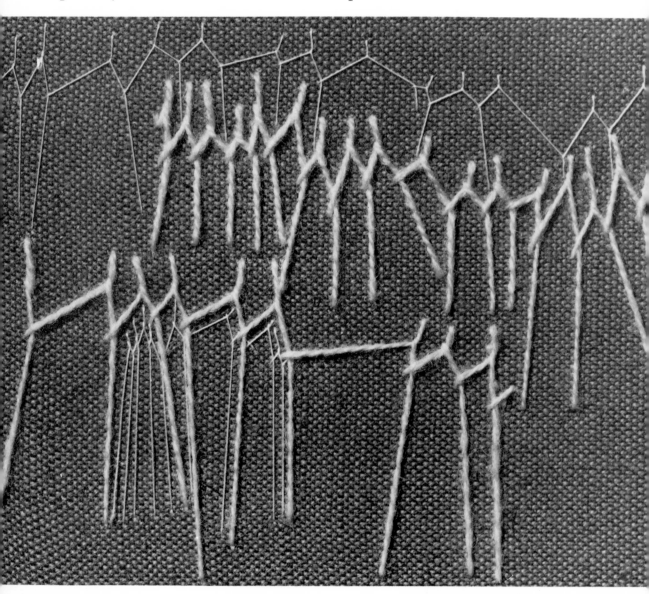

○ Can the stitch be structured into repeating patterns, interset or dovetailed?

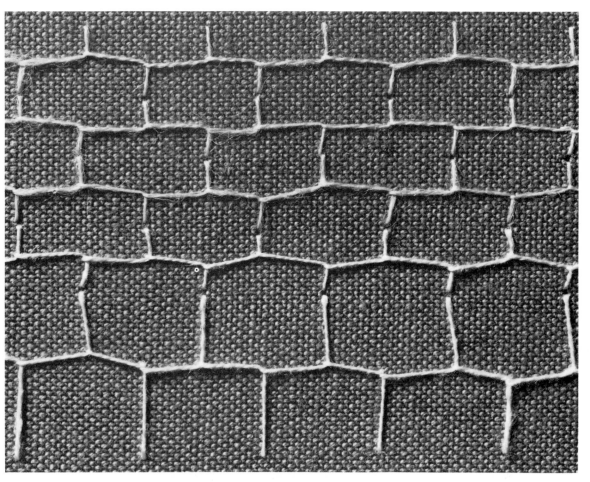

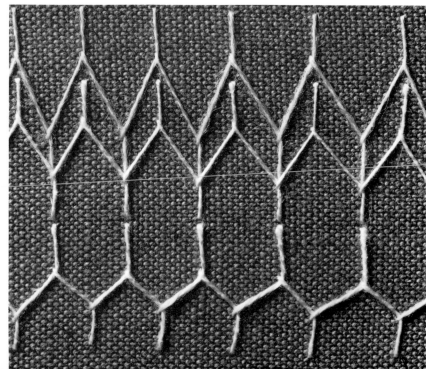

○ Can the stitch be worked as a solid area of texture or as
   a filling stitch?

Detail from an eighteenth-century skirt border. Cretan. (*Embroiderers'*
Guild Collection.)

'Landscape' worked entirely in cretan stitch in a variety of threads. (*Julia Barton*.)

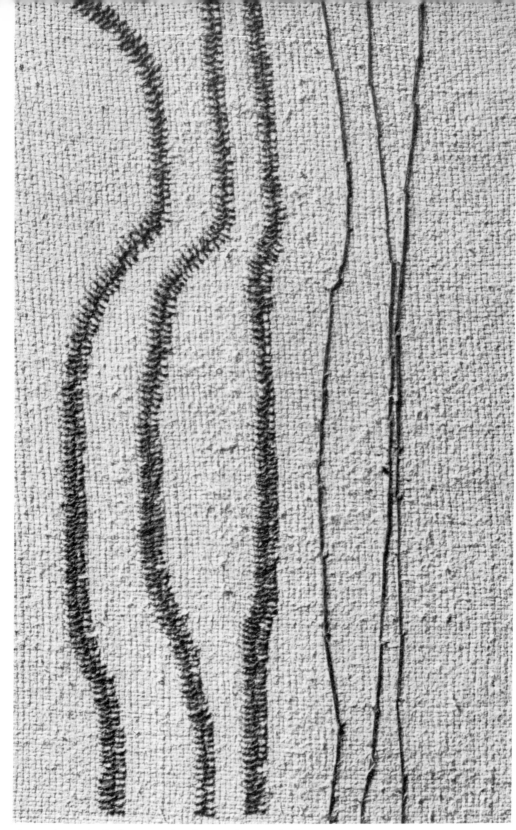

○ Can the stitch be worked as a line stitch?

○ Can the stitch be worked in circles?

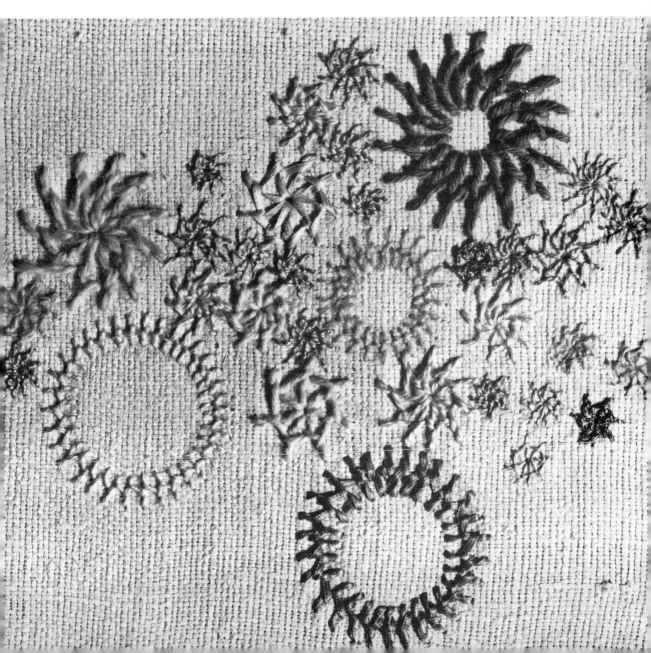

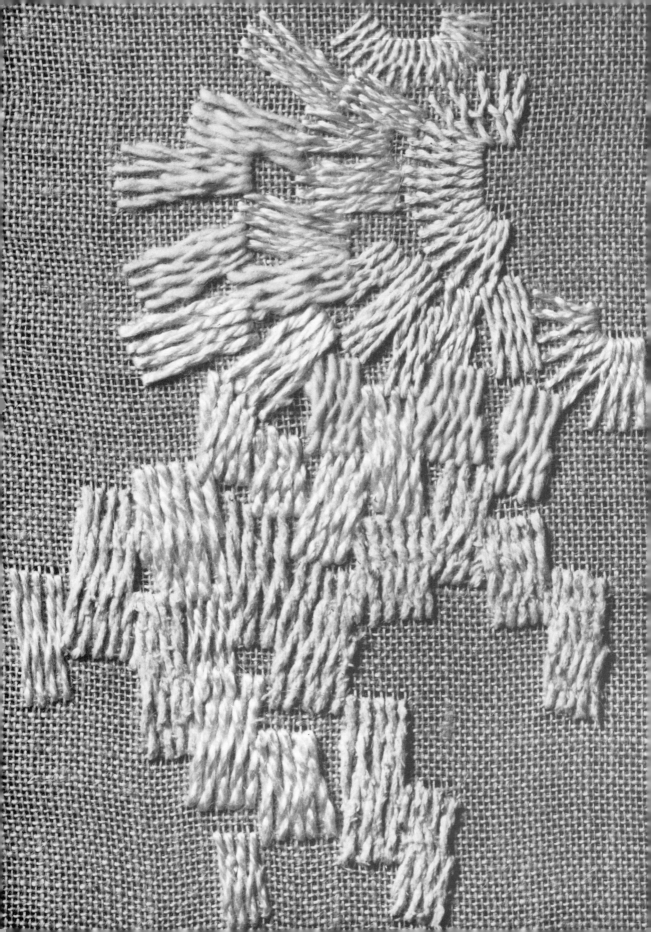

○ Work the stitch in blocks, twists, vertically . . .

○ . . . horizontally, upside down, diagonally – all directions!

Work the stitch in levels or layers. Overlap or encroach the stitch.

Grasses and wild flowers worked in layers of cretan stitch. (*Sheila Shaw*.)

○ Try working the stitch very tightly or in a very loose manner.

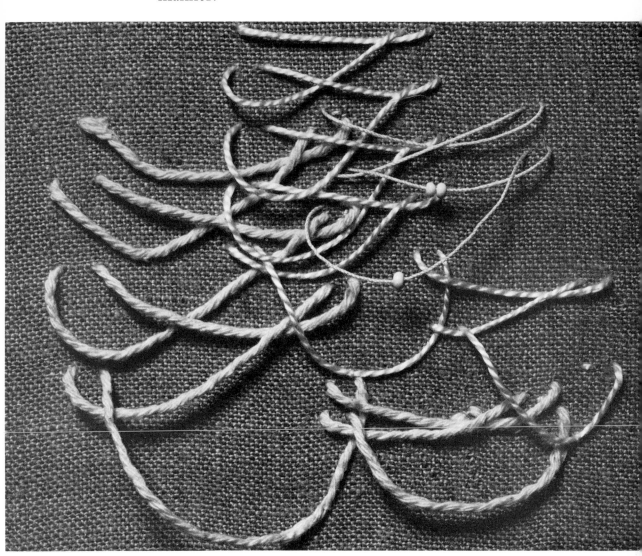

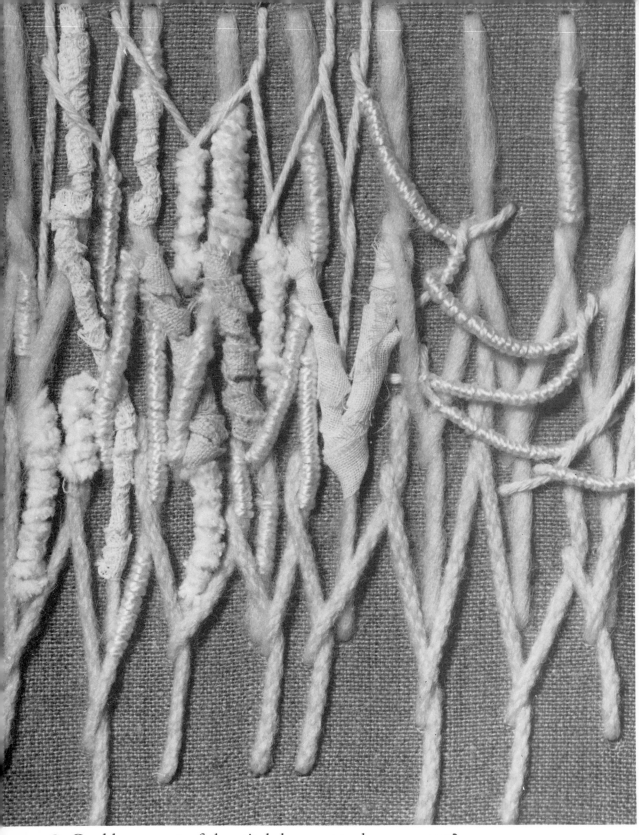

○ Could any part of the stitch be wrapped or overcast?

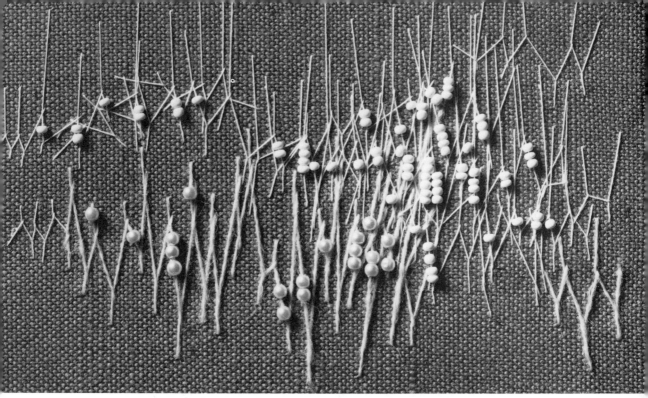

○ Can beads be incorporated during the work process?

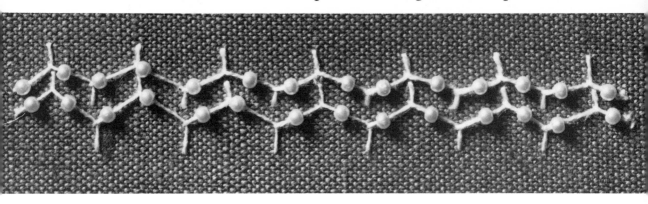

○ Consider whether plastic, wire, wood or fabric could be patched, looped, threaded or worked over the stitch.

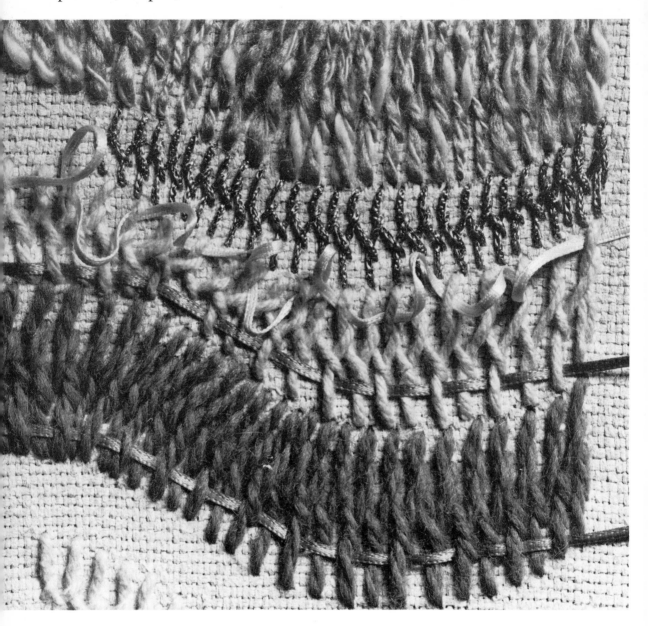

○ Can the stitch be worked over some form of padding or be padded after working?

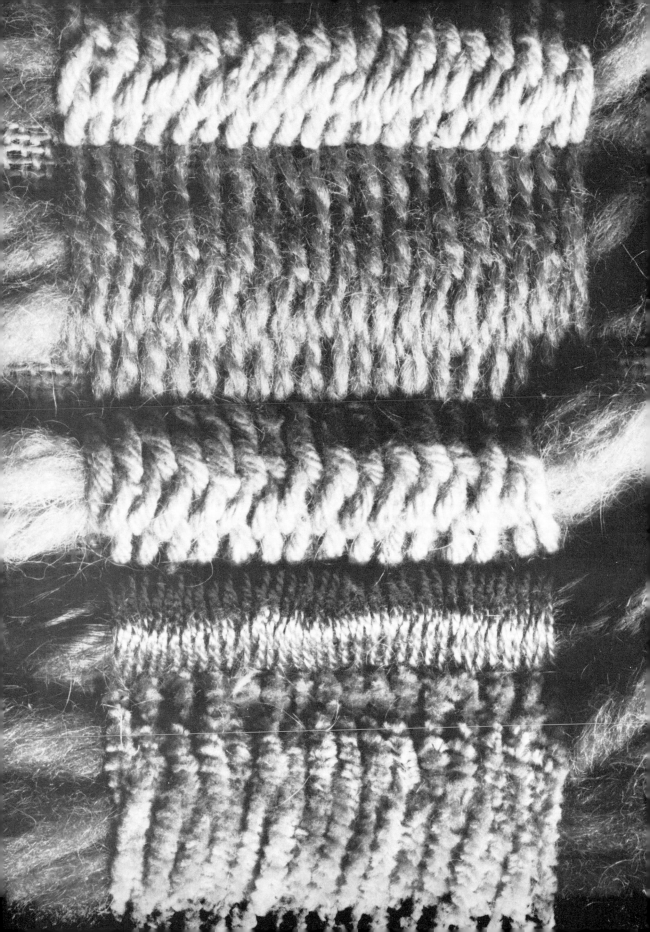

RAISED STEM
STITCH BAND

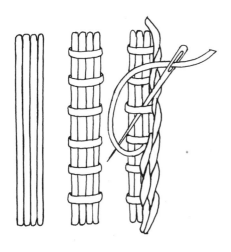

○ Work in a variety of threads. Try different threads on one needle. Cut fabrics into lengths and use instead of yarn. Try ribbons, tape and other decorative strips.

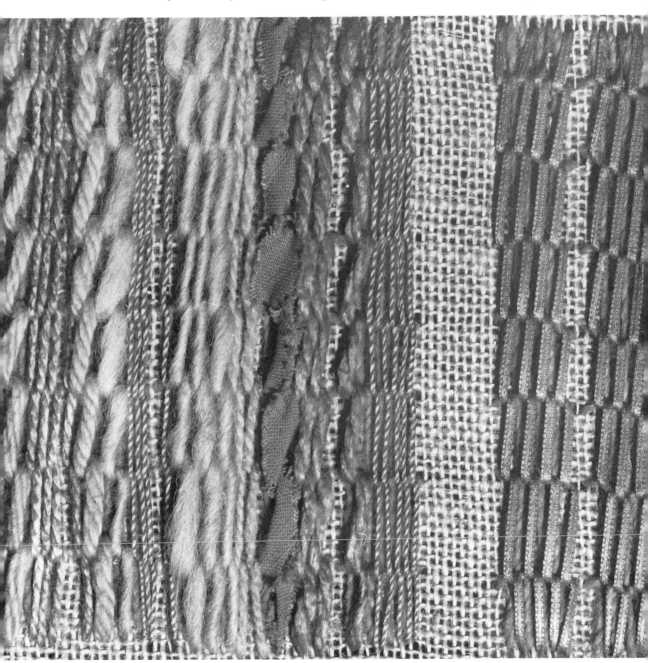

○ Try working the stitch in a long, thin manner.

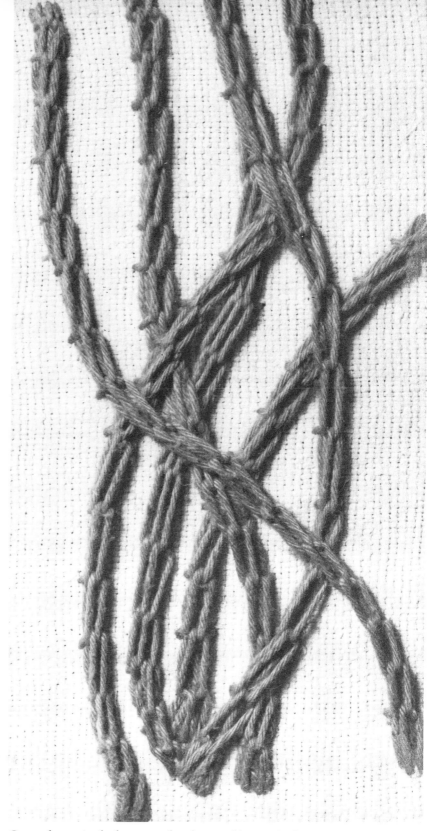

○ Can the stitch be worked as a line stitch?

○ Work the stitches very closely together.

○ Now try the stitch in a broad, 'stretched out' manner.

○ Work in thick and thin threads.

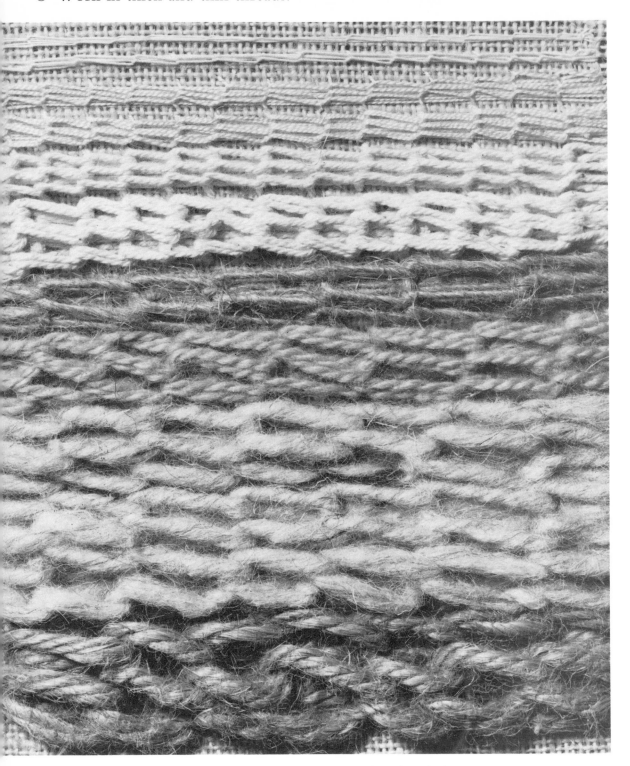

The example shows the stitch worked horizontally. Threads include
string, rug wool, macramé cord and coton perlé.

○ Can the stitch be worked to fill solid shapes?

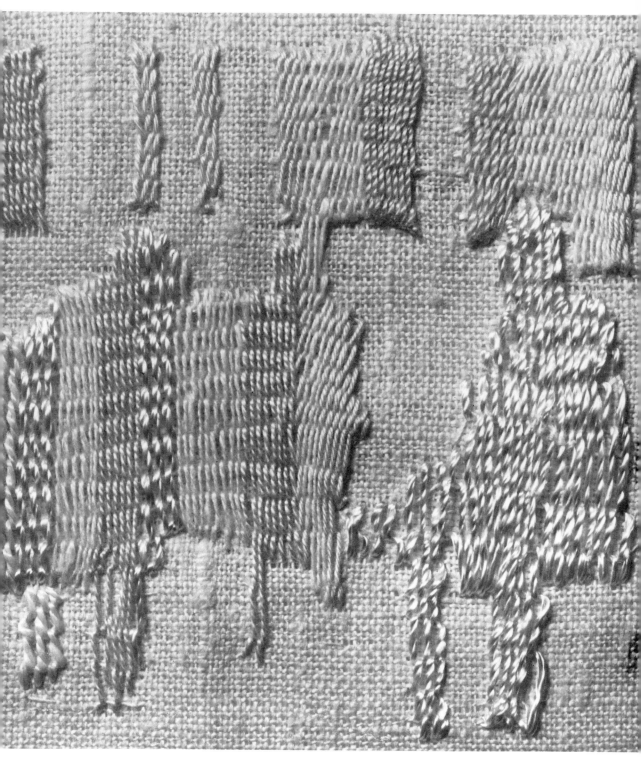

An interpretation of a group of figures, worked in shiny and matt yarns. (*Dorothy Wooding.*)

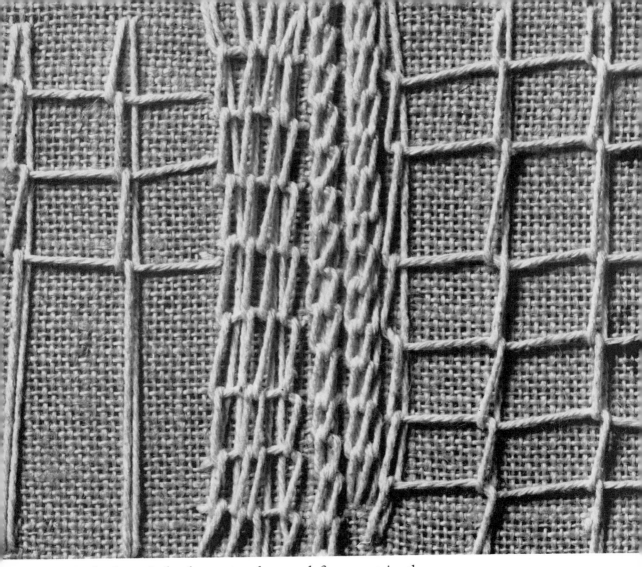

○ Work the stitch close together and far apart in the same pattern.

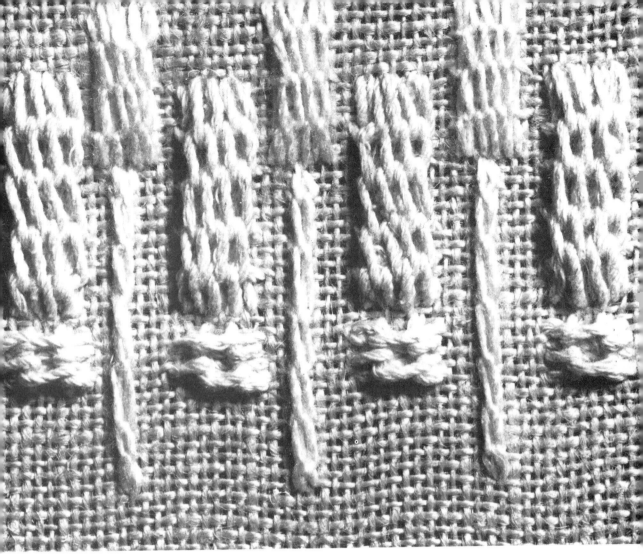

○ Work the stitch into repeat patterns, interlocking or dovetailing blocks of stitches.

○ Can the stitch be worked in circles?

Some of the stitches are partially worked showing the foundation stitch
couched in place ready for the stem stitch to be worked over the bars.

○ Can the stitch be overcast or wrapped with other yarns?

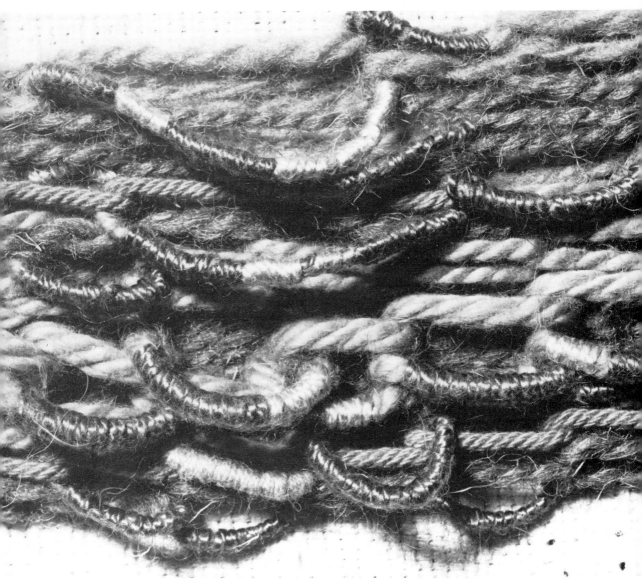

The bands of stitches have been worked horizontally with some of the stem top stitching wrapped with a shiny coton perlé.

○ Work the stitch in blocks, twists, spirals, diagonally or in
  all directions.

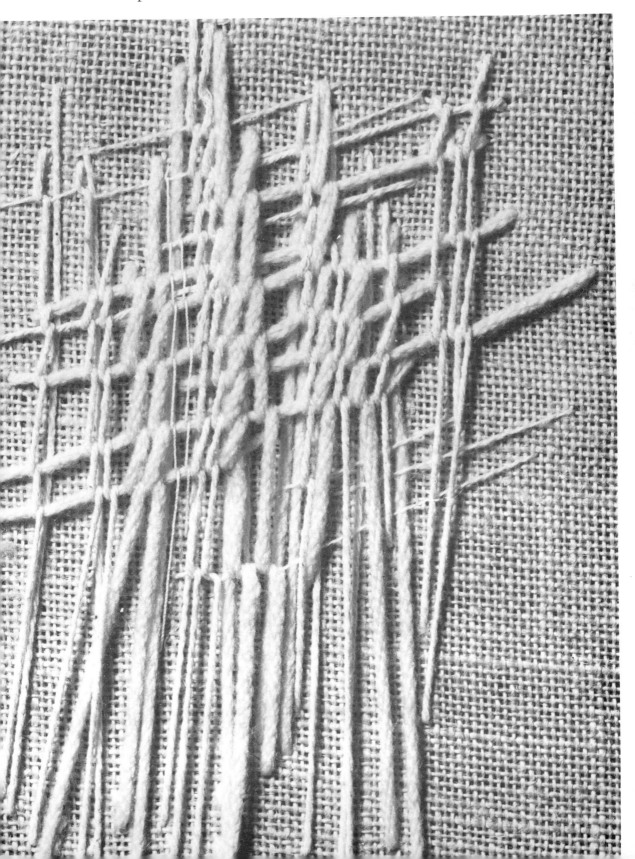

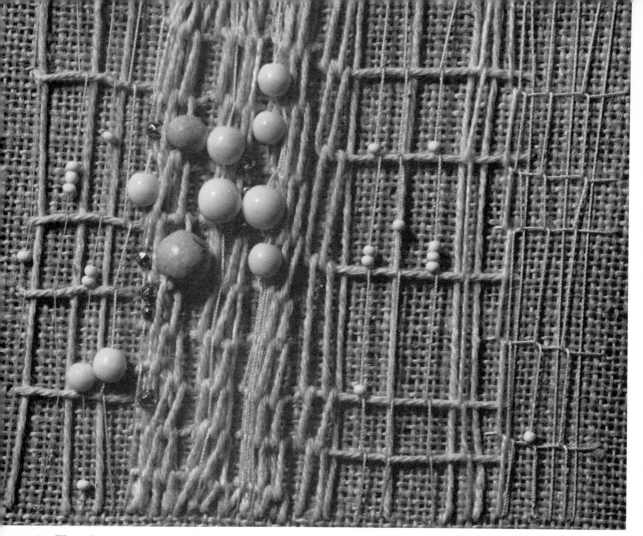

○ Try incorporating beads in the work process.

○ Work the stitch in levels or layers. Overlap or encroach the stitch.

○ Can the stitch be padded or threaded or laced with other materials?

○ What does the wrong side of any of the samples look
  like? Could any of the accidental textures be another
  starting point?

Looking at other stitches

The following section shows a number of stitches, each of which is illustrated by a diagram and a sampler worked in the orthodox way. Further examples show stitches of varying sizes worked in a range of yarns, and a number of the purely textural pieces illustrate how the stitch looks when different starting points have been considered. Other interpretations show the stitch developed further within a more considered design application. The textural permutations appear to be endless.

Note
Generally most samples are shown their original size whilst others have been slightly enlarged to enable the stitches to be seen more clearly.

The most usual name for the stitch has been used, with secondary names given in brackets. Care has been taken to limit the confusion, but stitch books of note often do not agree.

BACK STITCH
(Quilting stitch, Point de sable)

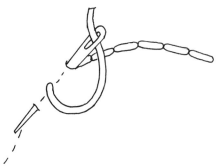

Lines of back stitch worked in thin, thick, matt and shiny threads.
Notice that some rows show the stitch worked loosely, giving a raised
effect. (*Mary Shea.*)

BACK STITCH WHEELS

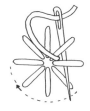

Back stitch wheels worked in smooth and textured yarns in a wide range of sizes. (*Gilly Wraight.*)

BULLION KNOT

(Caterpillar stitch,
Worm stitch,
Coil stitch,
Porto Rico rose)

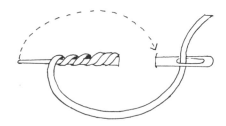

Detail of bullion knot filling (point rose) taken from a seventeenth-century crewel work hanging. Notice that the stitch has been worked in groups of three. (*The Embroiderers' Guild Collection.*)

Bullion knots worked in narrow ribbon on sequin waste applied to hessian. (*Pamela Lee*.)

Detail taken from an example of Mountmellick embroidery featuring bullion knots. Other stitches include buttonhole, coral and satin.

Knots worked with tails.

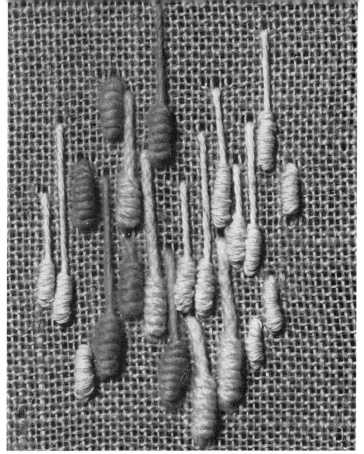

Bullion knots worked in the conventional way. Left: in a regular arrangement; right: in a haphazard way.

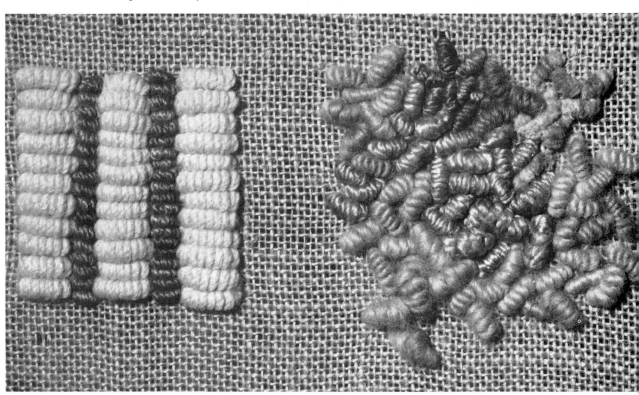

Knots worked deliberately unevenly, allowing the knots to unravel. All
samples worked in wool and cotton yarns.

'Beach Scene' worked entirely in bullion knots in a variety of threads.
The water's edge has been interpreted with the knots unevenly worked.
(*Pamela Lee.*)

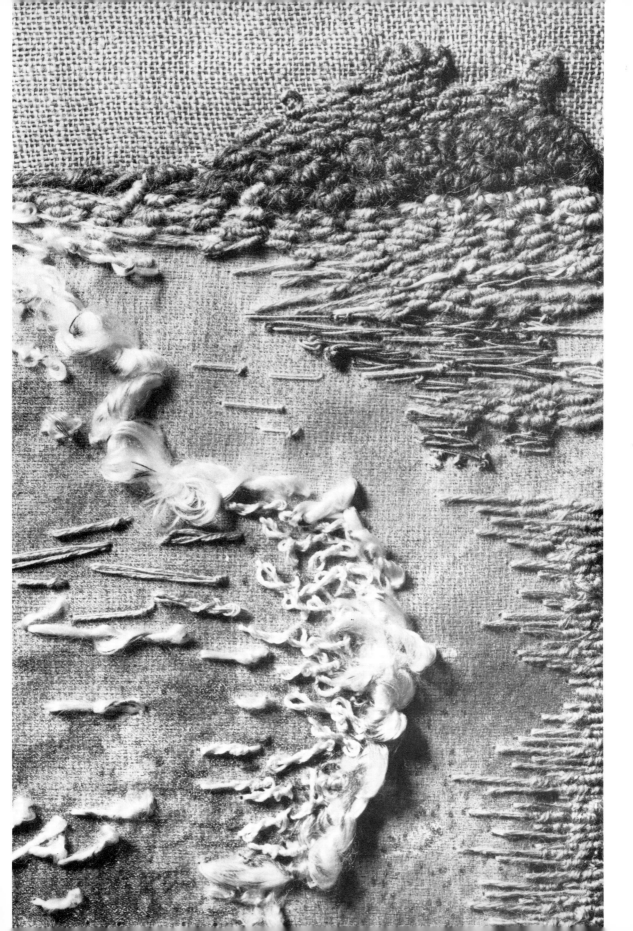

BUTTONHOLE STITCH
(Blanket stitch, Button stitch)

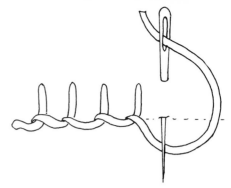

Rows of varying-sized buttonhole stitches worked in fabric strips,
ribbon, cotton and wool threads. (*Lizzie Ettinger.*)

An interpretation inspired by drawings of a quarry. Rows of close buttonhole stitches worked in matt and shiny threads. (*Ann Cunningham.*)

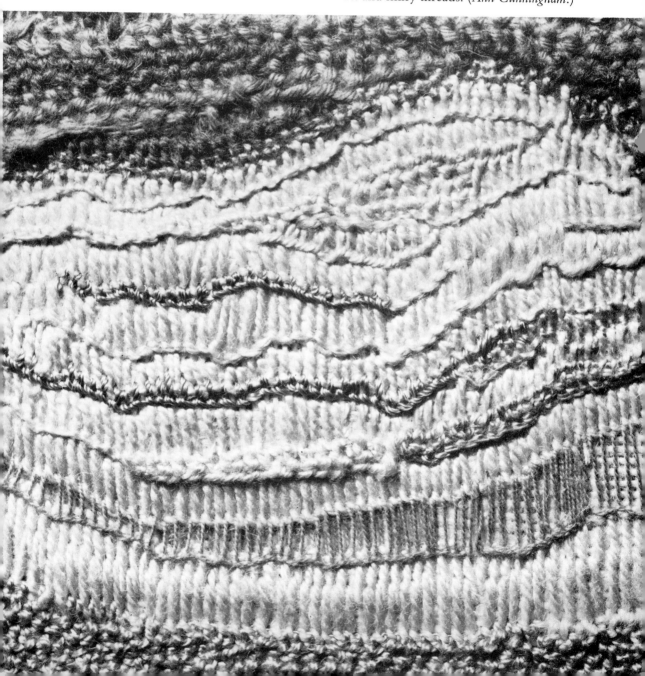

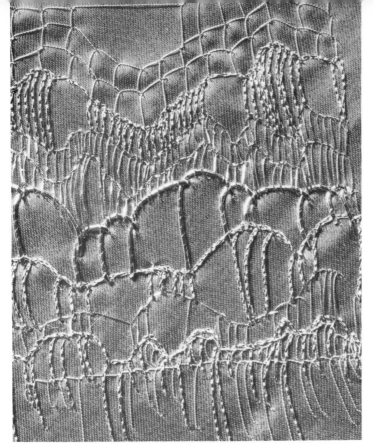

Open buttonhole stitches worked in thick and thin gold threads. The scale and placing of the stitches create interesting contrasts. (*Lizzie Ettinger.*)

Detail from a richly textured evening top. Lines of open buttonhole stitch and wheels worked in thick and thin threads. Flower-shaped pieces of fabric, sequins and ribbons have been incorporated in the design. (*Julia Caprara.*)

Stitch 'sketch' of trees worked in wools. (*Meg Wingham.*)

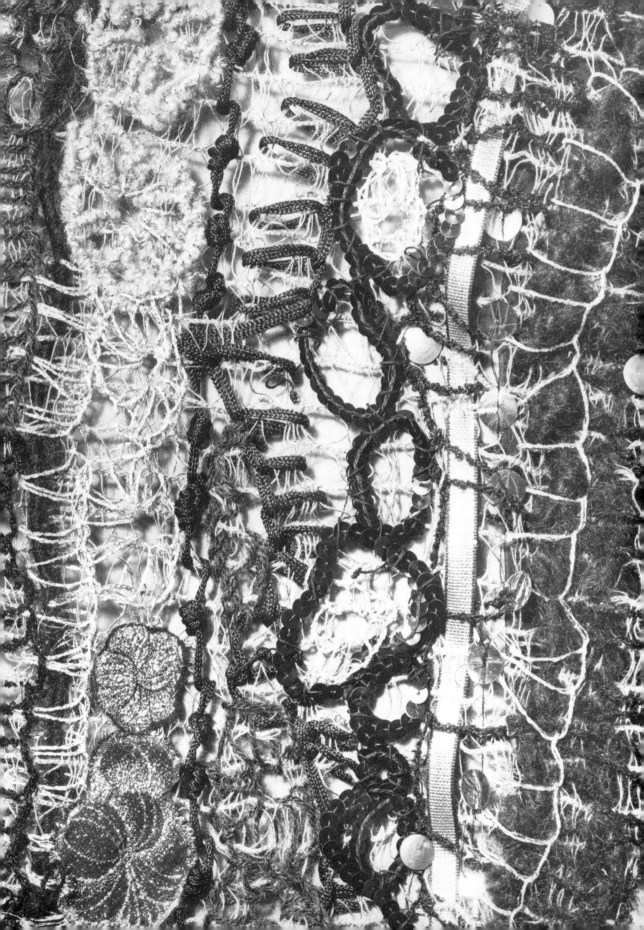

BUTTONHOLE STITCH – DETACHED

Work two straight stitches, bringing out the thread just above the left-hand end. Work buttonhole stitches over the bar only and not through the fabric. Take a small stitch into the fabric at the end of each row and then work a reverse buttonhole stitch into the looped edge of the previous line of stitches.

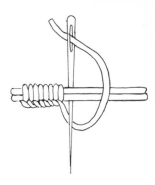

This interpretation of a section of tree bark was worked in a variety of threads. The foundation bars were worked in many directions and the threads were not anchored at the end of each row, enabling the resulting areas of stitches to be slightly rolled and sewn into position. (*Beryl Court.*)

Blocks of detached buttonhole worked in thick, thin, shiny and matt threads.

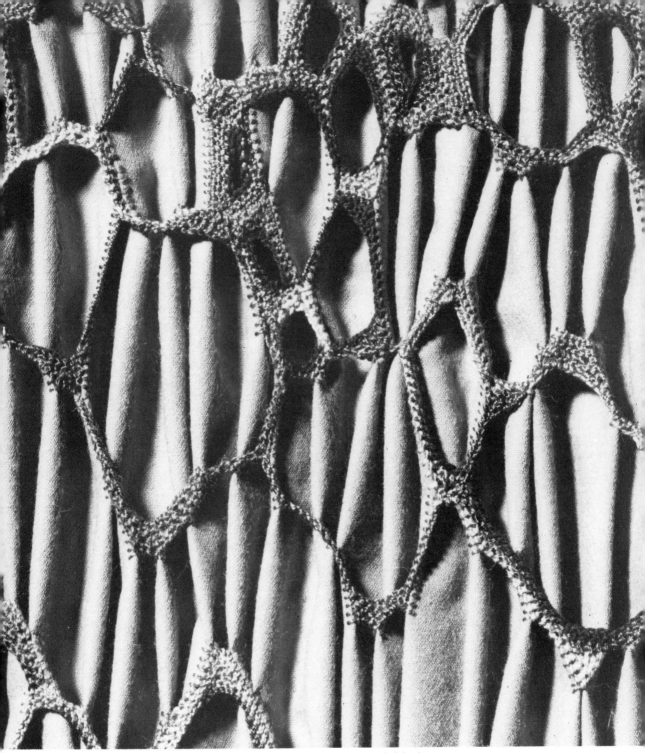

A detail from a pleated section of a coat dress. The stitch has been worked over the folds, forming a cellular effect. Coton perlé thread contrasts well with the matt fabric. (*Margaret Potts.*)

BUTTONHOLE STITCH – DETACHED (PICOTS)

(Ring picots)

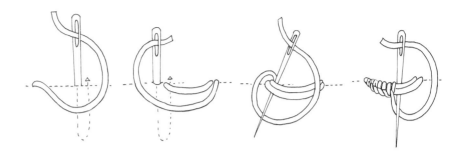

Small buttonhole picots worked evenly make a charming edging stitch. Other effects can be achieved by working the stitch in a thicker thread in a haphazard arrangement.

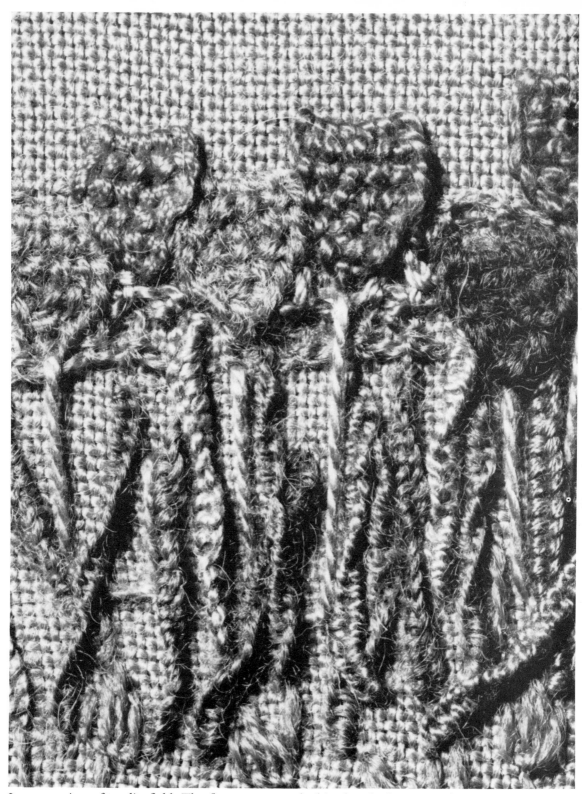

Interpretation of a tulip field. The flowers are worked in detached buttonhole and buttonhole picots. (*June Linsley*.)

BUTTONHOLE FILLING – KNOTTED

Work a row of running or back stitches around the shape to be filled to enable the buttonhole stitch to be worked over it and not through the fabric. For a freer interpretation vary the size and spacing of the top row of back stitches. Try not anchoring the stitch at the ends of the row and start the reverse journey directly into the last stitch. For a more lacy effect do not stitch into every loop. It is not always necessary to work the entire length of the row before reversing the procedure.

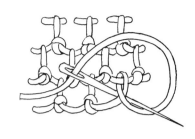

Evenly spaced stitches worked in crochet cotton, fine ribbon and thick cotton yarn.

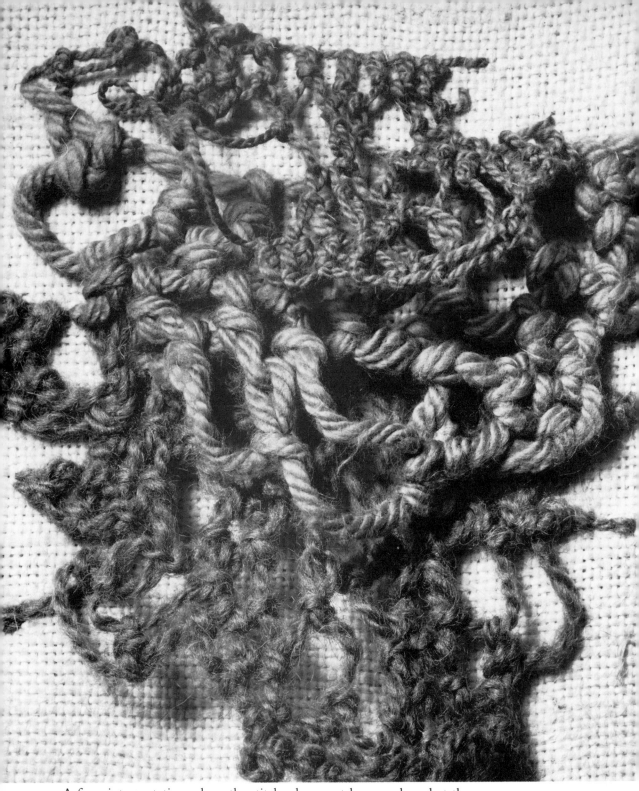

A freer interpretation where the stitches have not been anchored at the ends of the rows.

An interesting landscape scene worked entirely in buttonhole variations, the larger shapes in open buttonhole filling stitch. The design has been set into a machine-embroidered edging. (*Ann Sutton.*)

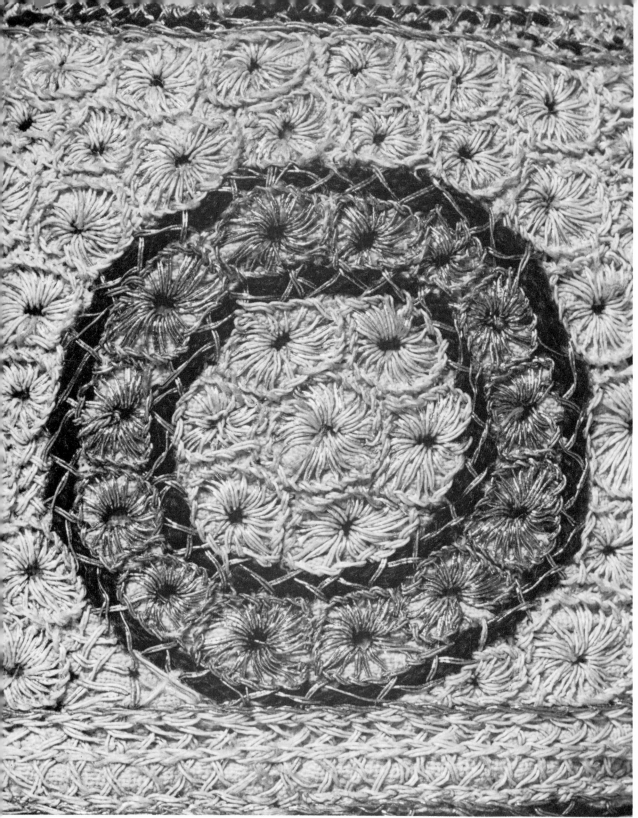

A detail taken from a man's cap worked mainly in metal threads. From Afghanistan, twentieth century. (*Embroiderers' Guild Collection.*)

BUTTONHOLE WHEELS
(Buttonhole circles)

Buttonhole stitch worked in circles. Notice that
the looped edges of some stitches have been
placed on the outer edge and others in the
centre. Some stitches have been worked on top
of others. Threads include wool, coton perlé
and coton à broder. (*Lizzie Ettinger.*)

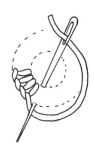

CHAIN STITCH

Chain stitch worked in a wide variety of yarns including wool, cotton, tubular rayon, macramé cord and textured weaving yarns. Notice how the loops and slubs affect the look of the stitch. (*Diana Siedl.*)

Rows of chain stitches worked in dishcloth cotton yarn. Long and short stitches have been worked within the same line; some stitches are quite loosely formed.

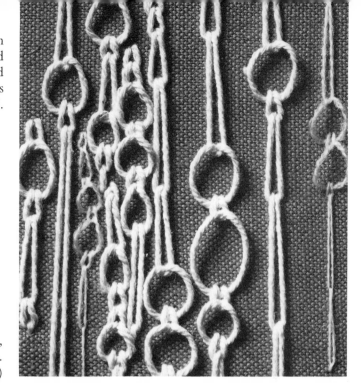

Random lines of chain stitch. Wool, cotton, ribbon and strips of bandage. (*Julia Barton*.)

Rows of varying-sized chain stitch, some of which have been worked
so loosely that large loops feature and contrast with the tighter stitches.

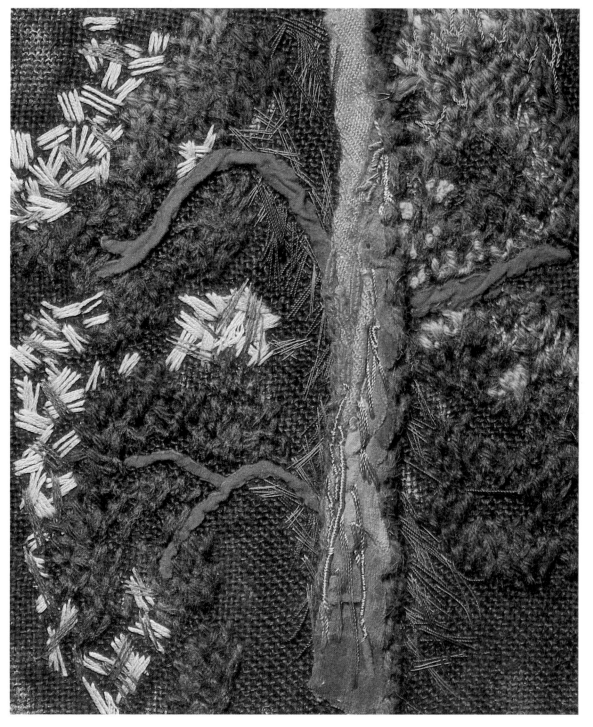

1 'Tree': appliqué, straight and fly stitches. *(Henrietta Curtis.)*

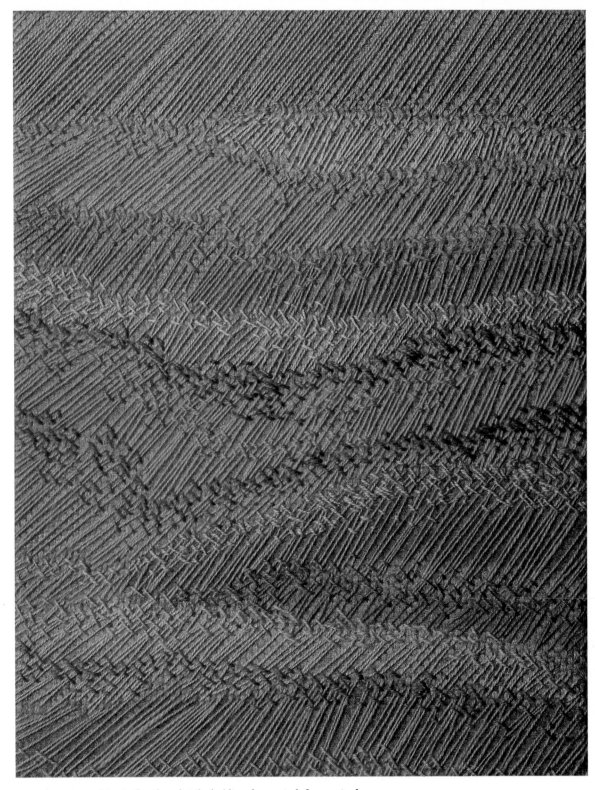

2 'Landscape': couching in fine threads. The holding down stitch features in the
design. *(Rosemary Jarvis.)*

3 'Bluebell Wood': worked entirely in cretan stitch. *(Evelyn Luxford.)*

4 Detail from 'Bluebell Wood': fabric strips couched down. *(Rosemary Jarvis.)*

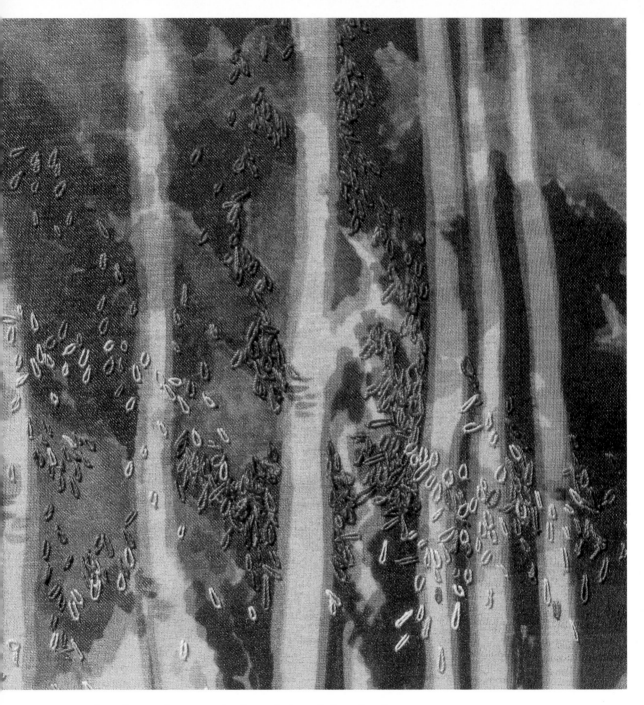

5 'View through Trees': design printed with transfer dyes. The leaves have been depicted in detached chain stitch. The stitches are in fine silk threads. *(Roy Hirst.)*

6 A section of tree bark interpreted in fly stitch worked in strips cut from nylon tights. *(Margaret Howells.)*

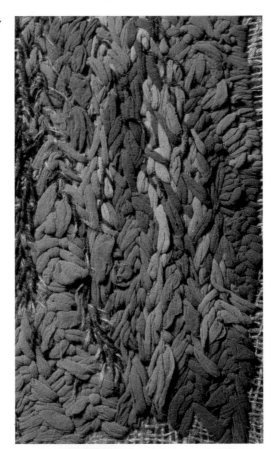

7 The surface of bark worked in textural stitches, including bullion and french knots. *(Eileen Evans.)*

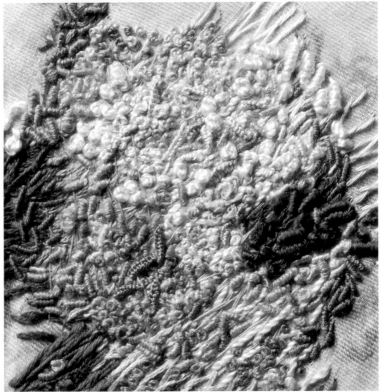

8 Detail from 'Life is Just a Little Bowl of Cherries': appliqué, straight and cross stitches. *(Audrey Walker.)*

9 'Flowers' depicted in thorn stitch. *(Jean Littlejohn.)*

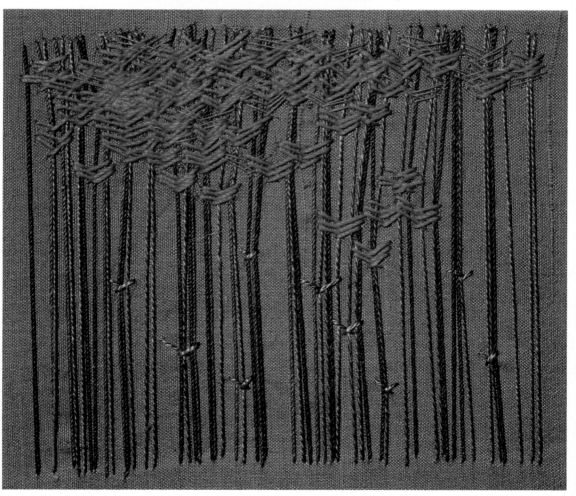

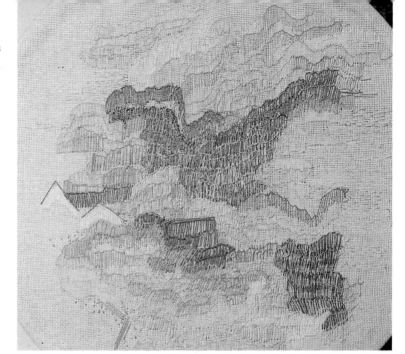

10 'Landscape – Stitch Sketch' worked in buttonhole stitch. *(Julia Caprara.)*

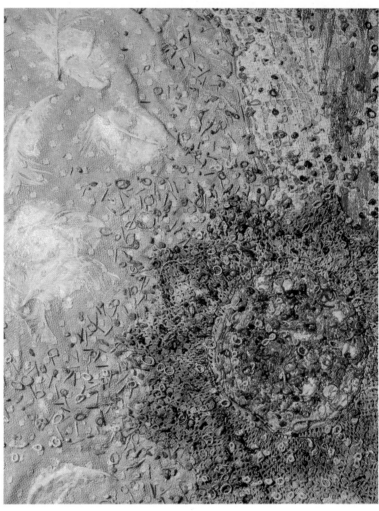

11 Detail from 'Colour Sound – Joy': appliqué, machine embroidery and hand stitches, including detached chain. *(Julia Caprara.)*

12 Detail from 'Clouds': straight stitches.
(Jean Draper.)

13 A design worked mainly in cretan stitch, on a skirt border. From Crete.
(Embroiderers' Guild Collection.)

CHAIN STITCH – DETACHED
(Lazy-daisy stitch, Daisy stitch)

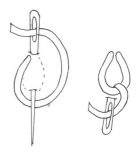

'Foxgloves' stitched with lengths cut from nylon tights, wool and tubular cord. (*Jane Clarke.*)

Left: overlapping stitches in shiny and matt threads. Right: blocks of regular-sized stitches worked in layers in parcel string.

A detail from a circular design
based on the Busby Berkeley
musicals. The figure is quilted and
decorated with couching and back
stitch. The feathers are depicted in
clusters of detached chain stitch
worked in shaded stranded cotton.
(*Ann Sutton.*)

CHAIN STITCH – KNOTTED CABLE

The diagrams are not the traditional method but a much rounder version.

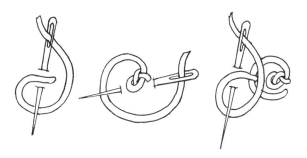

Rows of evenly spaced stitches worked in shiny braids and a coarse wool. (*Rosemary Jarvis.*)

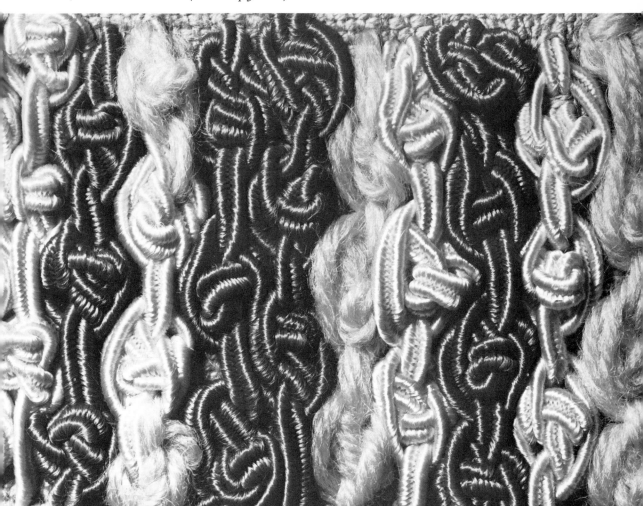

Knotted cable stitch worked in a wide variety of yarns including matt and shiny cottons, synthetic fibres, wools, fabric strips and ric-rac braid. (*Valerie Campbell-Harding.*)

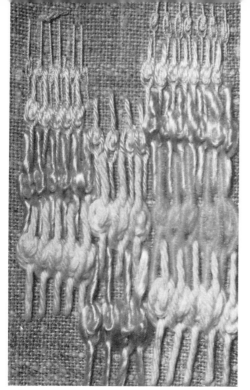

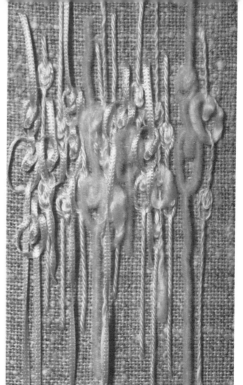

The stitch worked in overlapping clusters with long starting and finishing stitches, featuring wools, cotton and fine ribbons.

The stitch worked in groups of single stitches in a wide variety of threads.

Worked very loosely, so that parts of the stitch 'droop' down, giving an interesting effect. All samples by Valerie Campbell-Harding.

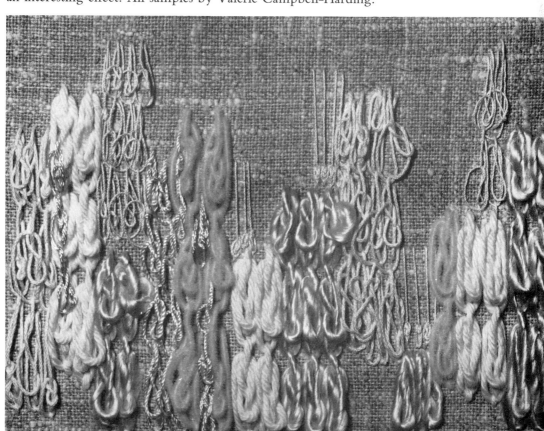

CHAIN STITCH – OPEN
(Square chain stitch, Ladder stitch)

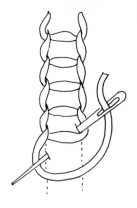

Open chain stitch worked in knitting wool, carpet thrums, coton perlé and metallic threads.

Circular motif worked in several layers of open chain in a range of threads. Ribbon has been threaded through the outer stitches to give a contrasting texture. (*Joan Tiley*.)

CHAIN STITCH – RAISED BAND

Raised chain band worked in wide range of threads including tubular cord, ribbon, fabric strips and hanks of yarn. Notice that the warp threads of the ground fabric have been used as foundation stitches. (*Ann Sutton.*)

Several layers of the stitch give a chunky surface. Wools, macramé
cord and thick cotton threads have been used.

Dishcloth cotton, slubbed weaving yarn and thick wool worked
unevenly over varying lengths of foundation stitches. (*Clare Emery.*)

Raised chain band worked with large spaces between each chain.
Metallic threads on canvas. Threads have been left to hang loosely at
the end of each row. (*Jill Grose.*)

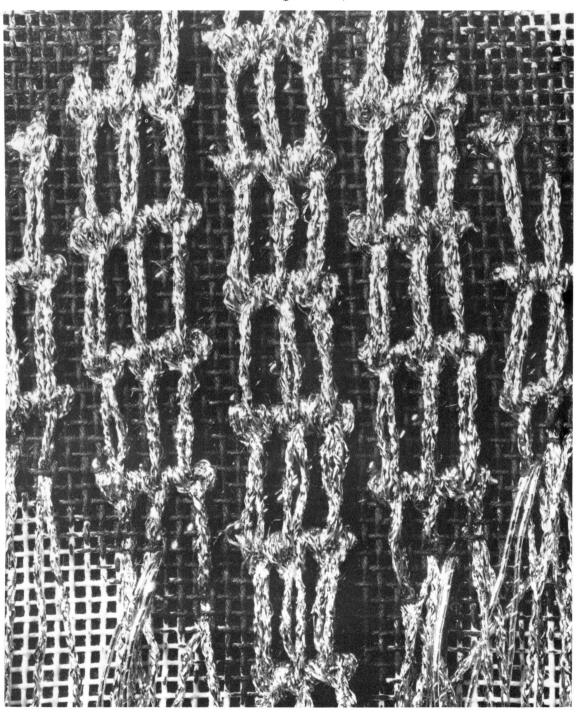

CHAIN STITCH – ROSETTE
(Bead edging stitch)

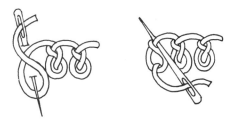

The stitch worked in a range of thick, thin, matt and shiny threads.
(*Ann Sutton.*)

Freer, uneven rows of stitches worked in dishcloth cotton, ribbon and chenille threads. Notice that some stitches have been worked on others and the bottom row of stitches shows the loop between the stitches featuring more prominently. (*Linda Crossling*.)

CHAIN STITCH – TWISTED

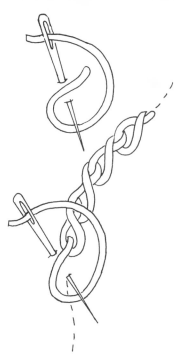

Twisted chain stitch in a variety of yarns including wool, silk and tape.

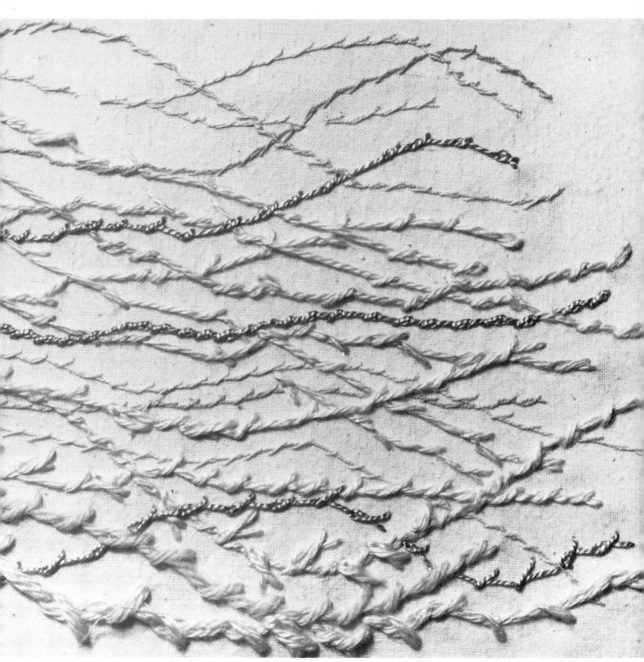

Finer lines of stitchery worked in soft embroidery and coton perlé.
(*Cherry Crawford.*)

CHAIN STITCH – WHIPPED

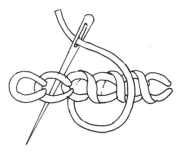

Fine and thick wool and cotton threads.
(*Margaret Potts.*)

Rows of chain stitch whipped and ▷
threaded with thin ribbons.
(*Margaret Potts.*)

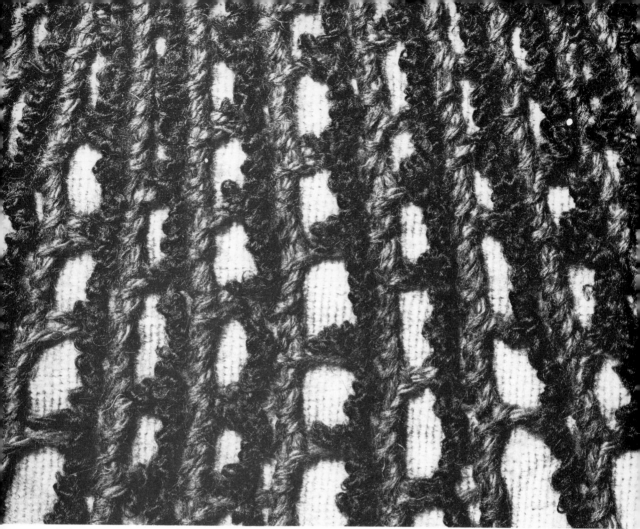

An interpretation of a ploughed field in knitting and textured wools.
(*Margaret Potts.*)

Landscape worked entirely in whipped chain stitch in a variety of yarns.
(*Margaret Potts.*)

CHEVRON STITCH

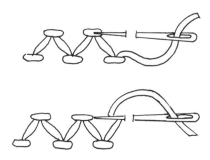

The stitch worked with uneven spacing. (*Kay Jackson.*)

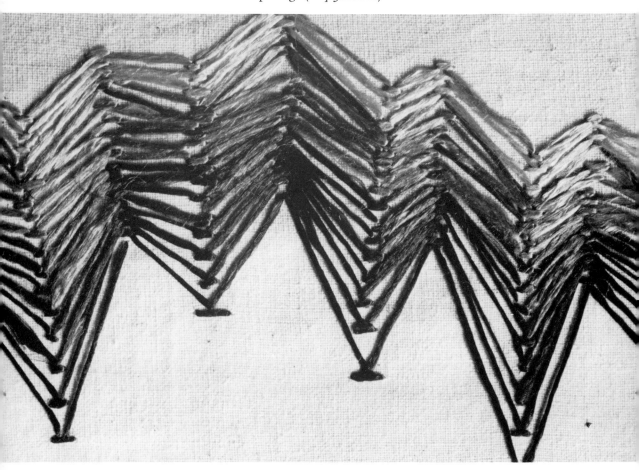

Chevron stitch worked in a variety of threads including weaving yarns,
chenille and ribbon. (*Kay Jackson.*)

'Landscape and Mountains' worked completely in chevron stitch in floss silk. (*Kay Jackson.*)

Pansies worked in chevron stitch in a variety of threads. (*Jenny Blackburn.*)

CHEVRON STEM STITCH

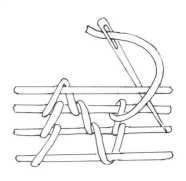

A bold pattern worked in thick wools and twisted threads.
(*Paula Templeman*.)

CORAL STITCH

(Raised stitch,
Coral knot,
German knot,
Snail stitch)

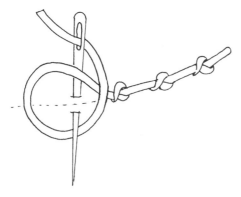
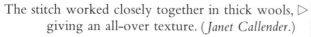
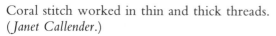

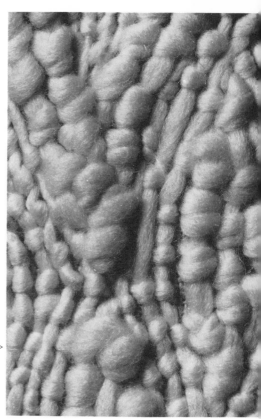

The stitch worked closely together in thick wools, ▷
giving an all-over texture. (*Janet Callender*.)

Coral stitch worked in thin and thick threads.
(*Janet Callender*.)

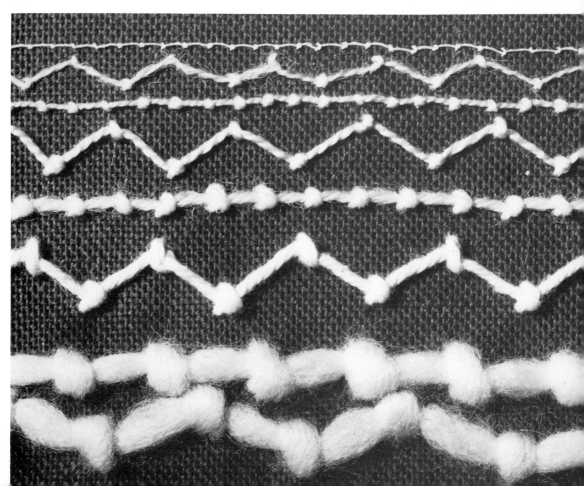

'Garden Scene' depicted entirely in coral stitch worked in a variety of directions. (*Janet Callender.*)

COUCHING

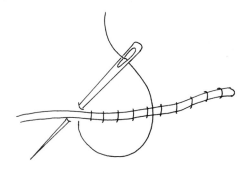

Rows of couched lines in a variety of thick, thin, matt and shiny threads. (*Rosemary Jarvis.*)

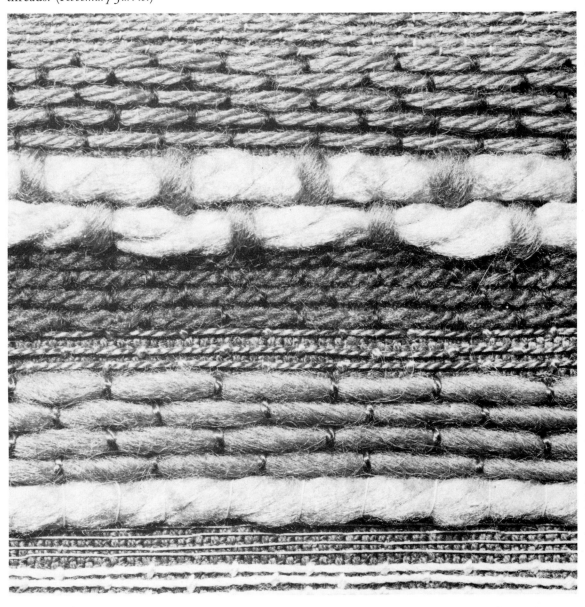

Figures depicted in continuous lines of couching in fine silk threads.
(*Molly Taylor.*)

Strips of felt couched down with coton perlé threads. (*Rosemary Jarvis.*)

COUCHING – BATTLEMENT

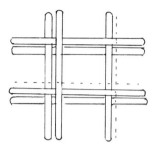

Lines of couching worked in layers to form grid arrangements. (*Beryl Taylor.*)

COUCHING – BOKHARA

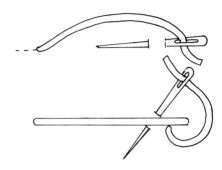

Couching worked in wool and cotton threads and fabric strips.

COUCHING – PENDANT

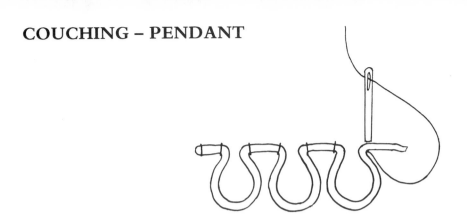

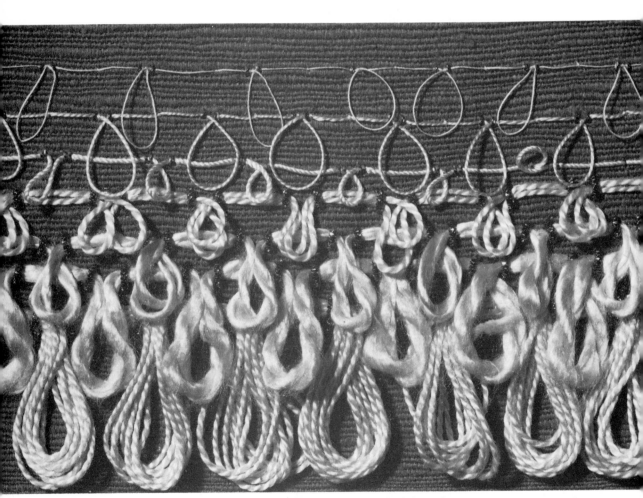

Lines of evenly worked pendant couching in thick and thin thread.
(*Ann Sutton.*)

An interpretation of a garden – couched spirals, pendant couching and [
short blocks of Roumanian couching. (This version is often referred to
as Roumanian stitch.)

An interesting surface made by mixed yarns, lace and fabric strips unevenly stitched in place. (*Rosemary Jarvis.*)

COUCHING – ROUMANIAN

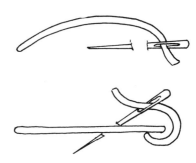

Roumanian couching worked in a range of wool and cotton threads, weaving yarns, ribbon and strips of chamois leather. (*Ann Sutton.*)

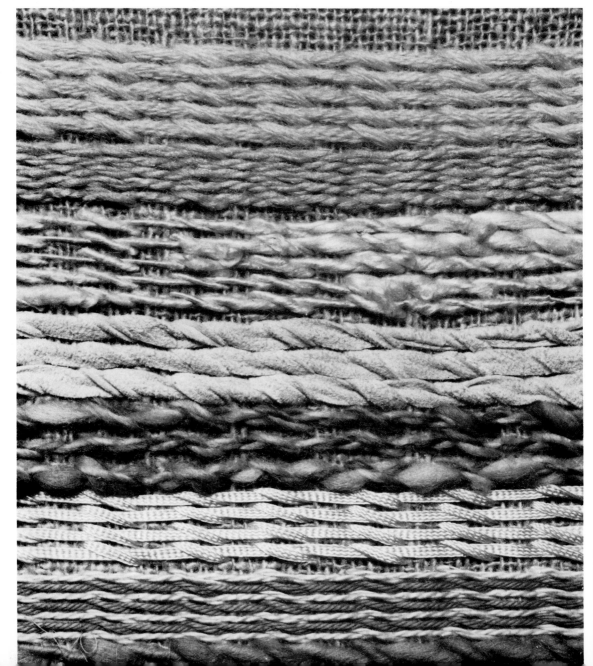

COUCHING – SATIN

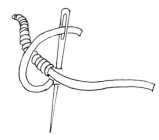

Various threads couched down with satin stitch. Interesting effects have been achieved by allowing the base thread to bulge through in places. (*Ann Sutton.*)

CROSS STITCH

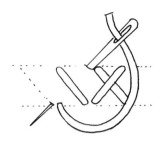

Simple figures depicted in cross stitch on linen. (*Elsebeth Just.*)

Section from a panel depicting flowers. Worked entirely in layers of various-sized cross stitches. (*Maria Wetherall.*)

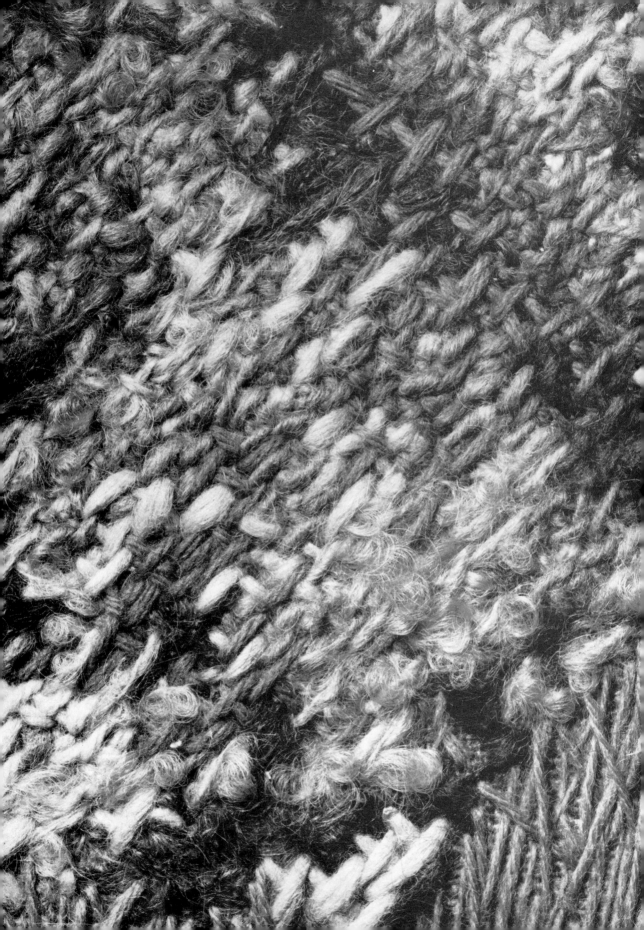

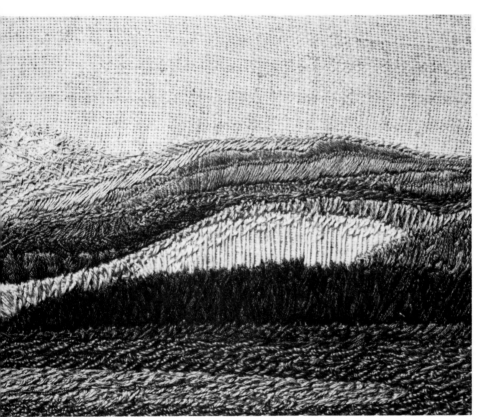

An interpretation of a landscape scene. Some cross stitches are worked haphazardly, others in rows with uneven spacing. (*Jean Jennings*.)

A figure depicted in blackwork on evenweave linen. The tonal ▷
variations have been produced by cross stitches worked in thick and
thin threads. Back stitch has been used for the outline.
(*Ann Cunningham.*)

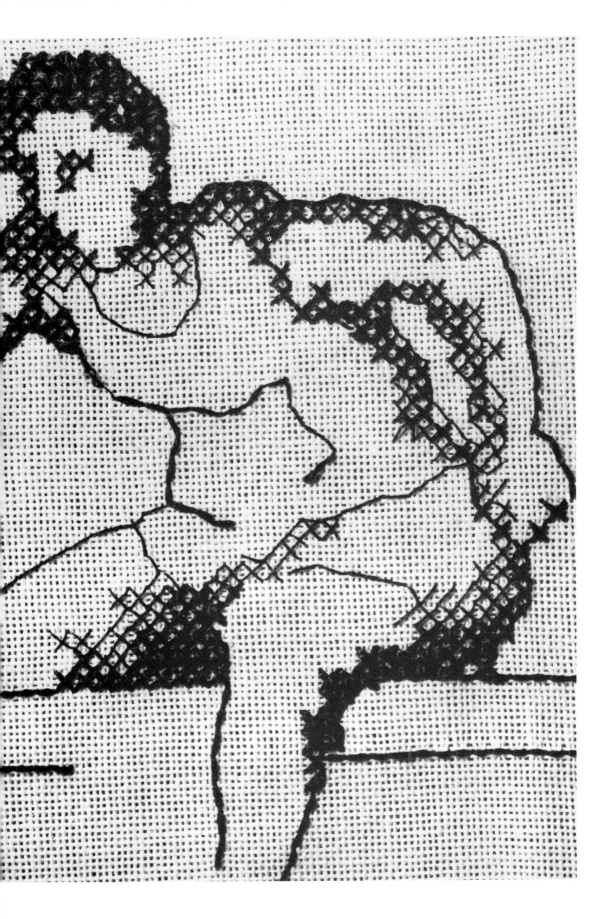

DOUBLE KNOT STITCH

(Palestrina stitch, Smyrna stitch,
Knot stitch – double)

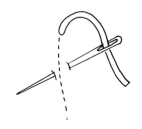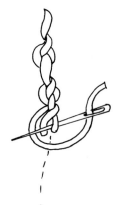

Double knot stitch worked in the conventional way in a wide range of
threads including strings, raffene and novelty yarns. (*Jean Lloyd.*)

Thick sisal string worked in several layers and threaded with a finer,
metallicized thread; an exciting surface with deep channels between rows.
(*Jean Lloyd.*)

An interpretation of a section of a heavily ridged tree bark. A variety
of string and leather strips have been incorporated in the design. Some
stitches have been worked one on another. (*Jean Lloyd*.)

EYELETS

The diagrams show the method of working an eyelet on closely woven fabric. Those worked on loosely woven materials can be achieved by taking the stitches into the same hole; the threads should be easy to pull in whichever direction is required.

Detail from a Hungarian bonnet; eyelets worked in brightly coloured cottons. (*Embroiderers' Guild Collection.*)

A charming interpretation of a brick wall, which was printed with dye and the flowers worked in tiny eyelets, the foliage in straight stitches. (*Jane Sweetsur.*)

Detail from a man's cap from Afghanistan. (*Embroiderers' Guild Collection.*)

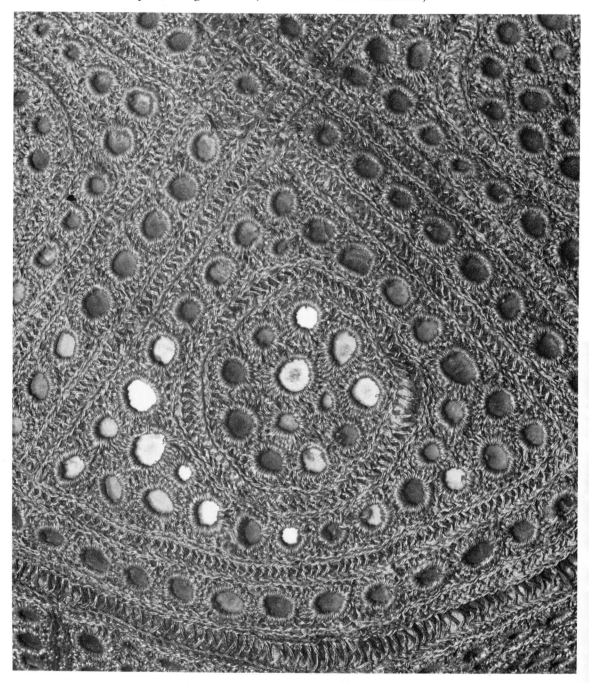

Detail taken from a three-dimensional fabric stone. The textural surface has been worked in random blocks of raised chain band with eyelets between. (*Jill Friend.*)

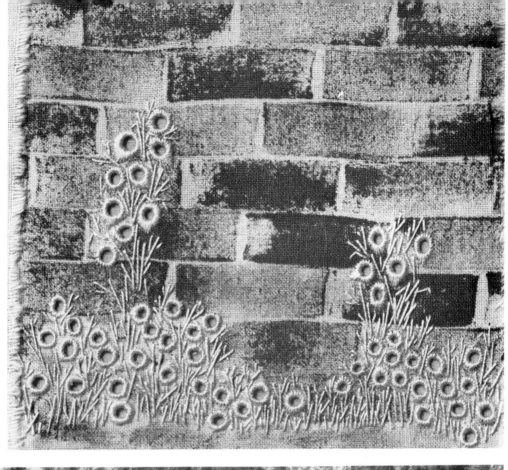

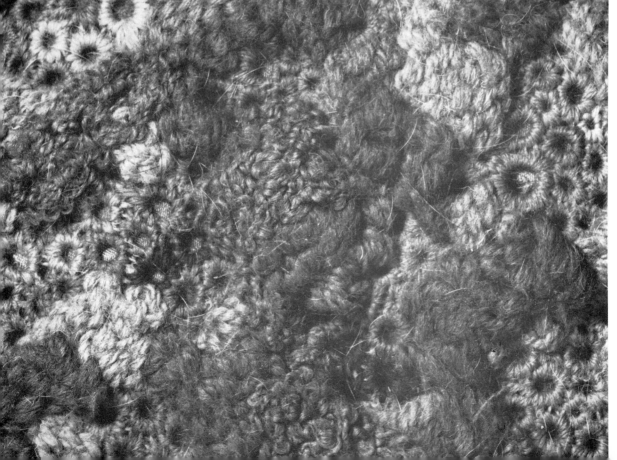

Various-sized eyelets worked in wool on a loosely woven fabric. The asymmetrical arrangement gives an interesting surface. (*Shirley Crawford.*)

'Daisies' worked as eyelets in raffene and encrusted with beads. (*Shirley Crawford.*)

FEATHER STITCH

Feather stitch worked in a broad manner: the ▷
amount of fabric picked up in each stitch is
greater than normal. Wool, rayon and cotton
threads. (*Beryl Taylor.*)

Rows of feather stitch worked in a range of
threads, ribbons and fabric strips. Notice the effect
of the stitches which have been worked with a
slack tension. (*Jeanne Turner.*)

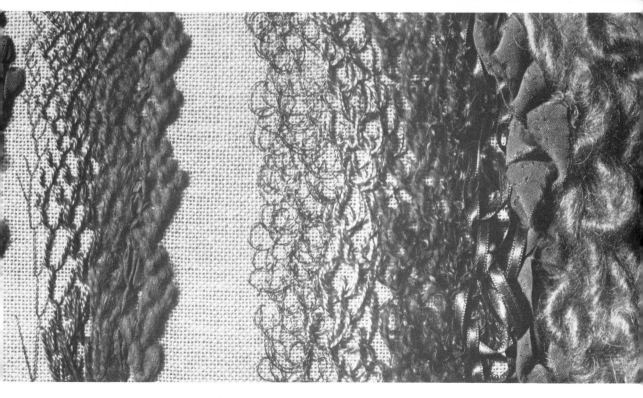

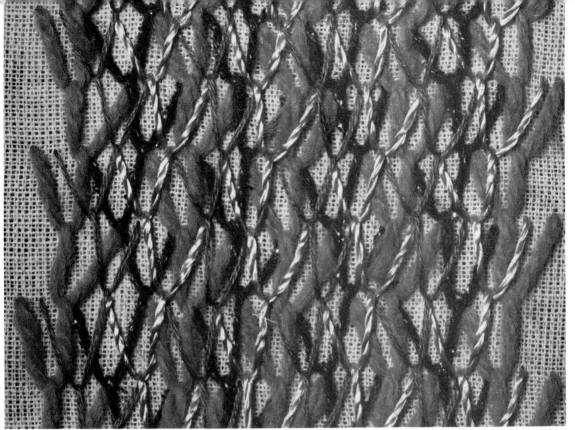

Rows of overlapping feather
stitch in matt and shiny threads.
(*Beryl Taylor.*)

Several layers of feather stitch
worked in wools, weaving yarns
and fine ribbons on millinery net
applied to a silk fabric.
(*Phyllis Gunstone.*)

Diagonal rows of encroaching ▷
feather stitch worked in perlita/
perlé and wools. (*Julia Barton.*)

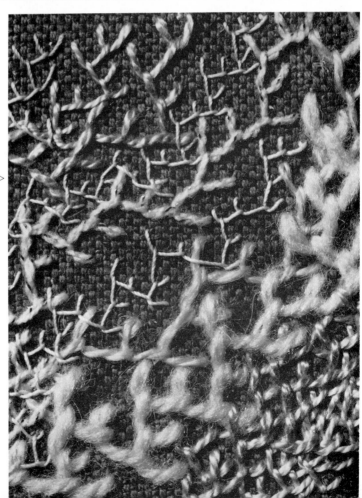

FEATHER STITCH – SPANISH KNOTTED

The stitch worked in dishcloth cotton, knitting wool and coton perlé.

14, 15 Details from two panels, both showing machine embroidery enriched by hand stitchery. *(Jean Littlejohn.)*

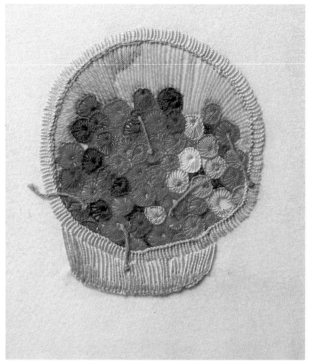

16 'Bowl of Cherries' worked in
buttonhole stitch. *(Lizzie Ettinger.)*

17 A section from a carpet worked totally
in chain stitch. From Baghdad.

18 *opposite* Detail from
'Changing Images': appliqué, machine
embroidery and straight stitches.
(Jan Beaney.)

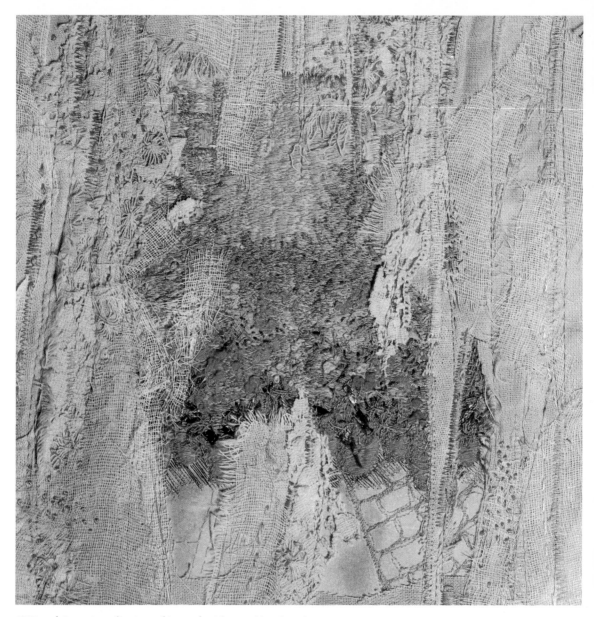

19 'French Image': appliqué, machine embroidery and hand stitches
(Jean Littlejohn)

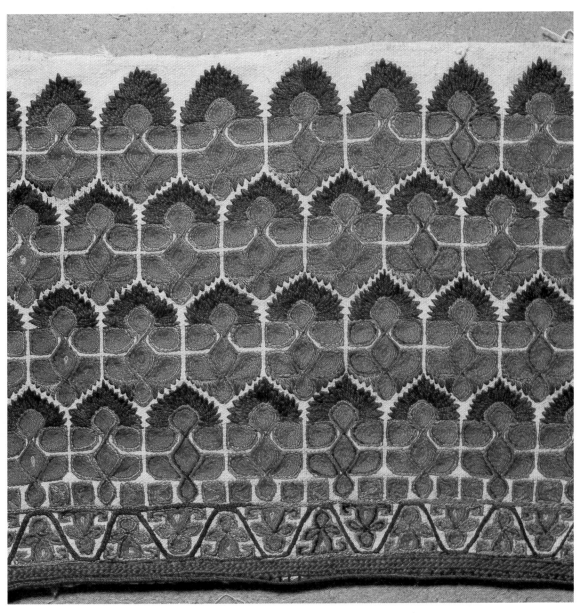

20 A repeat pattern worked mainly in solid stem stitch with some straight stitches. From the Balkan States. *(Embroiderers' Guild Collection.)*

21, 22 Two details from 'There's a
Rainbow Round my Shoulder':
appliqué, machine embroidery and
straight stitches. *(Audrey Walker.)*

23 *opposite* Detail from 'The Tree':
straight stitches in crewel wools.
(Eirian Short.)

24 *opposite* Detail from 'Colour Sound –
Coming Together': cross stitches and
straight stitches in thread and fabric
strips. *(Julia Caprara.)*

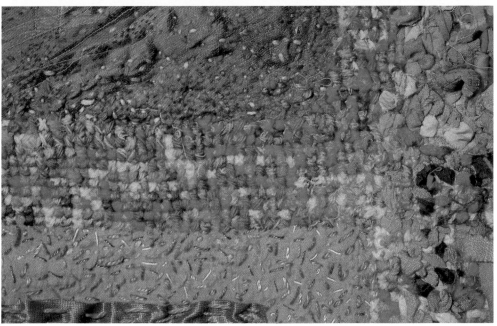

25 A section from 'Thrift and Daisies': cretan stitch in silk thread.

FLY STITCH

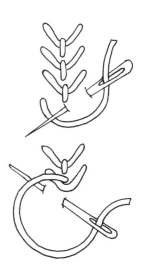

Two variations of fly stitch:
(a) with long holding down stitches

(b) worked closely together making petal or leaf shapes.

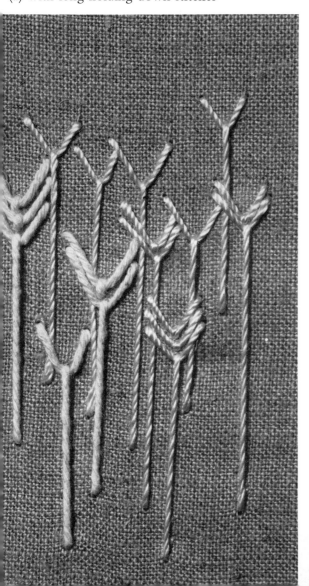

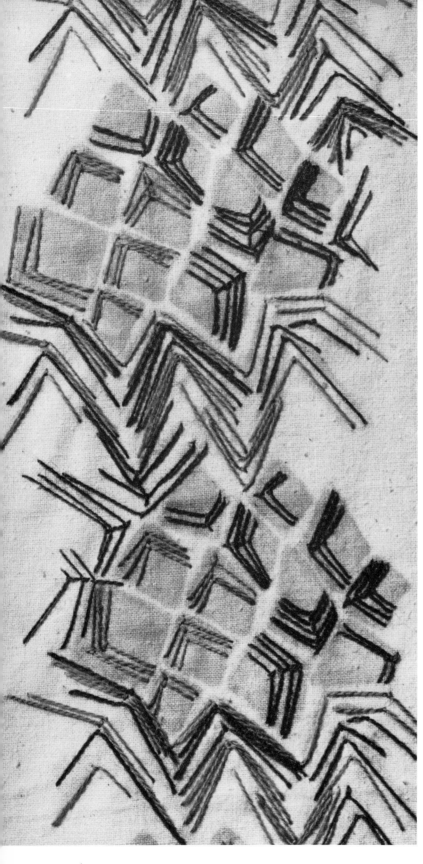

Simplified patterns inspired by blackberries. The base shapes have been printed with transfer dyes and emphasized with fly stitches worked in all directions. (*Jean Littlejohn*.)

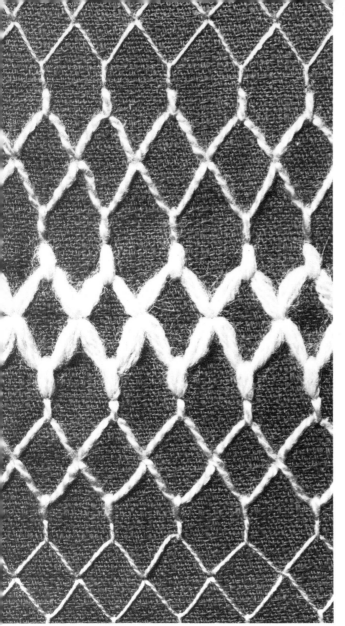

The stitches worked to form a repeat pattern in thick and thin threads. (*Margaret Howells*.)

A freer interpretation showing groups of overlapping stitches worked in sewing cotton, perlé, knitting and weaving yarns.

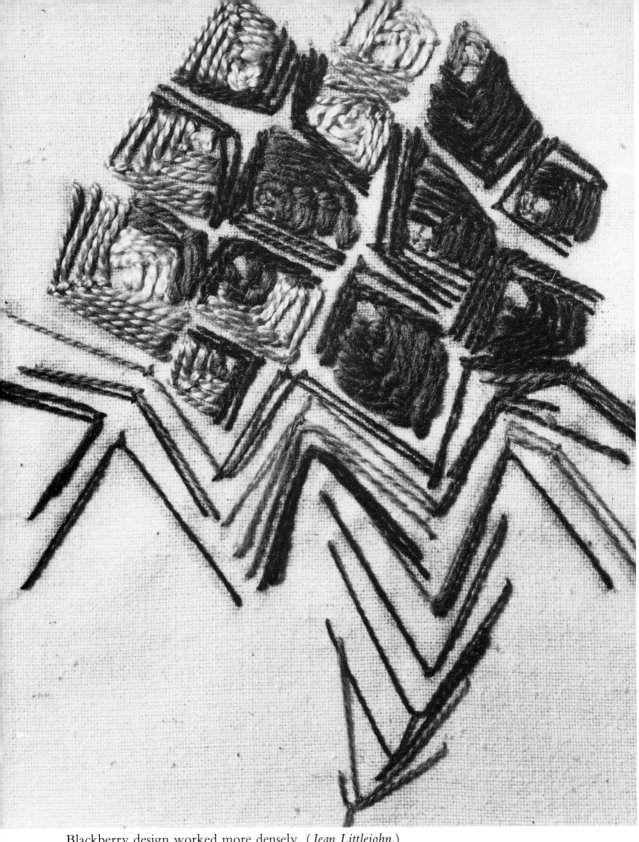

Blackberry design worked more densely. (*Jean Littlejohn*.)

FRENCH KNOT

(French dot, Knotted stitch, Twisted knotted stitch)

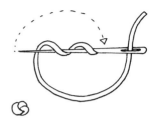

French knots worked in a variety of thick, thin, matt and shiny threads:
Top left worked conventionally
Bottom left with 'tails'
Top right not pulling the knot through properly, allowing a loop to feature
Bottom right incorporating beads

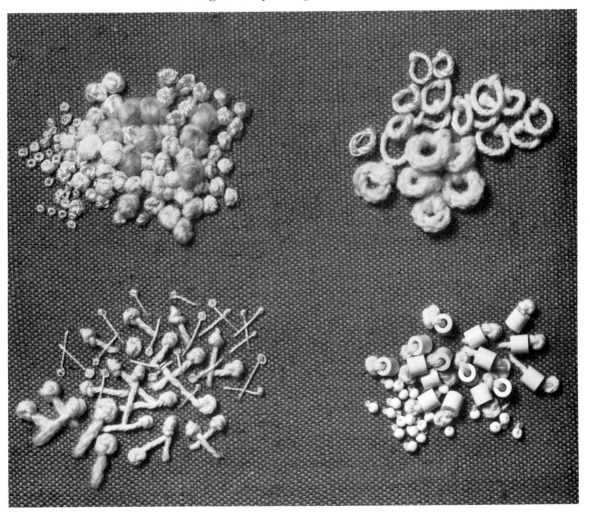

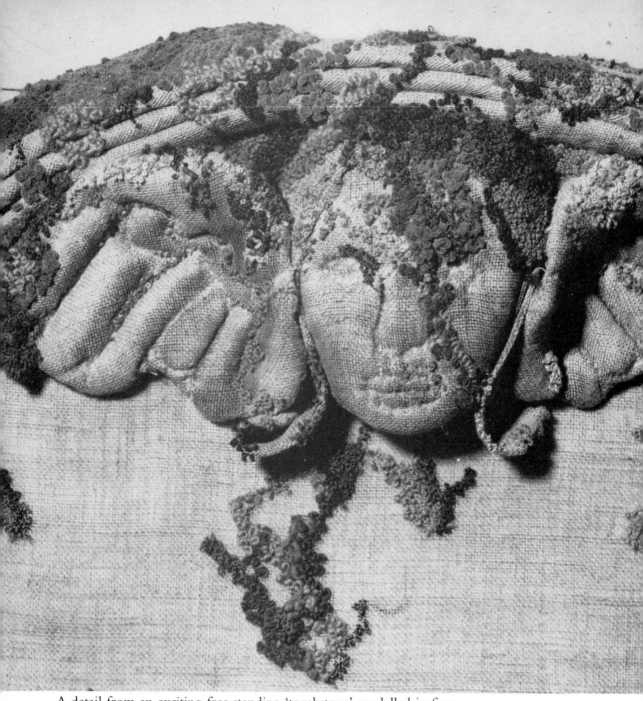

A detail from an exciting free-standing 'tombstone' modelled in fine scrim. Lichen and moss textures have been interpreted in areas of large and small french knots in cotton, wool and chenille. (*Phil Palmer*.)

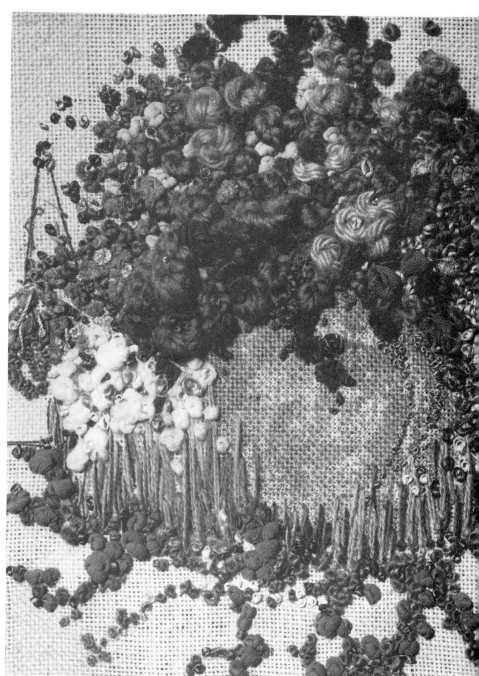

A section from a picture depicting a large pot of flowers standing in a cobbled courtyard. Layers of knots in a wide range of threads. (*Sheila Read.*)

Detail from 'Come Dancing' worked in crewel wools. (*Eirian Short. Photo: Denys Short.*)

HERRINGBONE STITCH
(Russian cross stitch, Russian stitch)

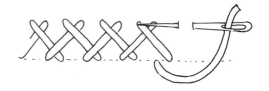

An animal motif worked in herringbone stitch in stranded thread. Mexican.

The stitch worked in circular patterns in fine threads. (*Margaret Suckling.*)

A haphazard arrangement of herringbone stitch worked in layers. Many yarns have been used, including bandage and fabric strips. (*Julia Barton.*)

Rows of encroaching herringbone stitch with wool laced through the stitches. (*Margaret Suckling*.)

Fragment from a cover. Jannina embroidery, eighteenth century. (*Embroiderers' Guild Collection*.)

LOCK STITCH

Rows of unevenly spaced lock stitch worked in white dishcloth cotton yarn, thin leather and calico strips. (*Margaret Rivers.*)

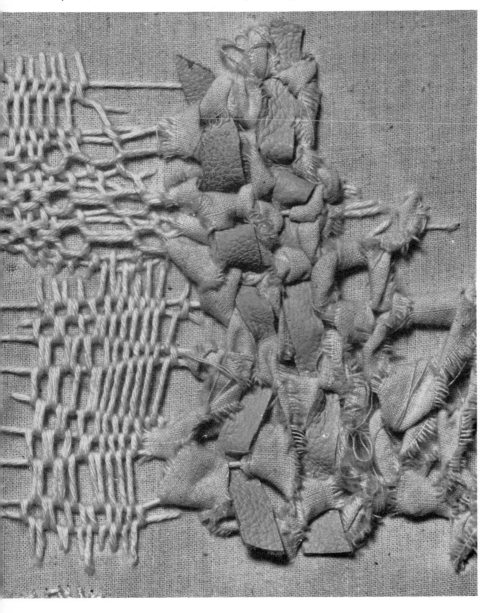

Lock stitch worked in the orthodox way in a range of thick and thin threads. (*Cynthia Waymouth.*)

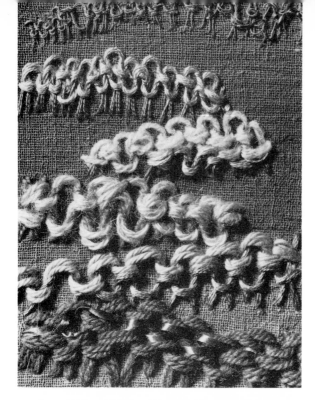

A freer use of the stitch interpreting a garden scene. Varying threads have been worked loosely and unevenly over the base stitch. (*Cynthia Waymouth.*)

The stitch worked to form a circular motif. Wooden beads have been incorporated in the stitch process. (*Margaret Rivers.*)

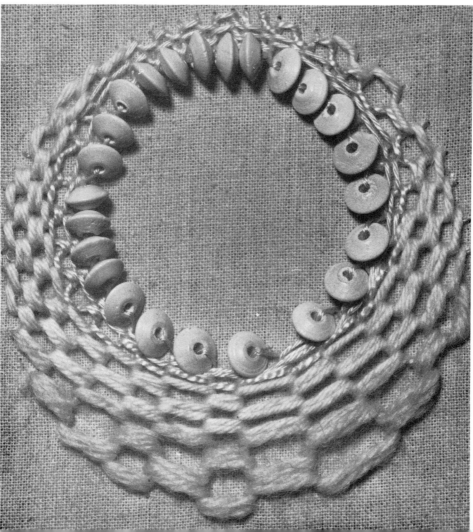

PEKINESE STITCH
(Chinese stitch)

Pekinese stitch worked in a range of threads including slubbed weaving yarns. (*Ann Sutton.*)

The stitch worked in thick cords on canvas. Notice the contrast of matt and shiny yarns and the change of scale. (*Sonia Cook*.)

A sea scene in Pekinese stitch. Fine, even stitches are worked at the top; fabric strips, lace and polythene in the foreground. (*Sonia Cook.*)

PORTUGUESE BORDER STITCH

Work the required number of foundation straight stitches. Commence at A with the thread to the left of the needle and carry it over and under the first two bars twice and then under the second bar only. Repeat this procedure for the length of the foundation bars without going into the fabric. Fasten off. Commence the left-hand side at B.

Rows of Portuguese border stitch worked in the orthodox way in a variety of yarns including wools, perlita, string and braid. (*Ann Sutton.*)

A small picture worked entirely in Portuguese border stitch. The interesting and very textural frame is worked in a range of yarns including gold braid and string, some of which was sprayed with gold paint. (*Ruth Levy.*)

SPLIT STITCH
(Kensington outline stitch)

Lines of split stitch worked in thin and thick threads including wool, cotton and fine ribbon. (*Jenni Last.*)

STEM STITCH
(Crewel stitch, Stalk stitch)

Stem stitch worked in a variety of threads including ribbon and lengths cut from nylon tights. (*Beryl Court.*)

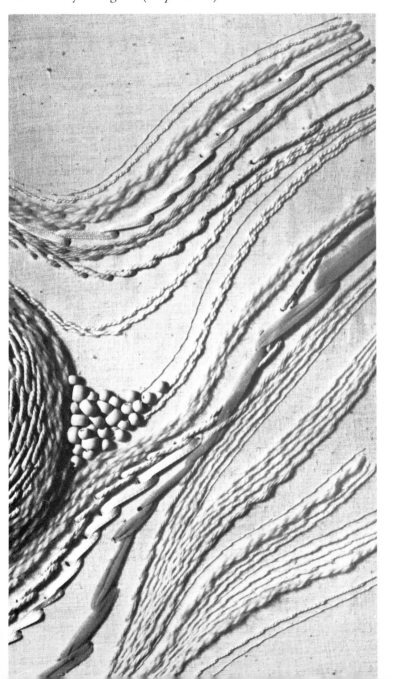

Stem stitch worked on a piece of free smocking. Beads have been incorporated in the work process. (*Ann Marchbanks.*)

STRAIGHT STITCH – SEEDING

Small running stitches worked in all directions.

An attractive design showing the effective use of running and straight stitches. French knots on the hat show a contrasting texture. (*Ann Sutton.*)

Haphazard running stitches worked on a semi-transparent fabric. Notice the varying effects created by the density of the stitches and the choice of the ground fabric. (*June Linsley.*)

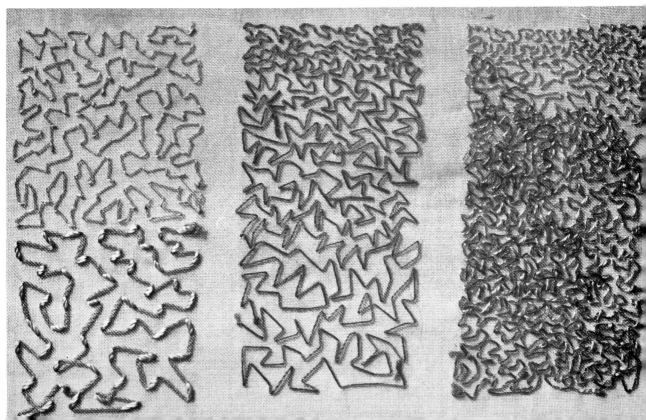

'The Threat of Birds', a panel worked in small, running stitches.
(*Elaine Waller*.)

Detail from 'Pearly King and Queen of Fulham'. Notice how the running stitches have been arranged to give particular effects. (*Kay Lynch*.)

Detail from 'There's a Rainbow Round my Shoulder'. Areas of seeding contrast well with the longer stitches. (*Audrey Walker.*)

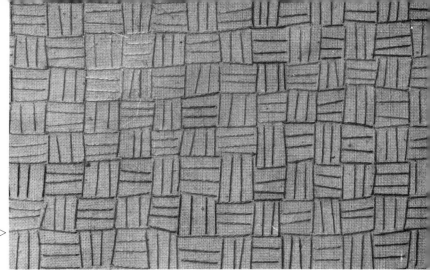

A simple pattern made from ▷ blocks of straight stitches. (*Annabel Brown.*)

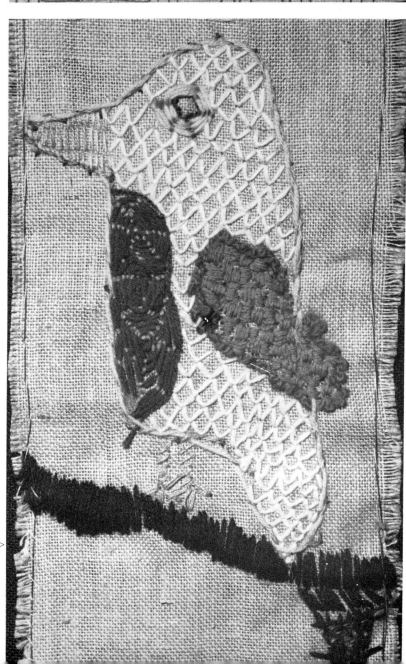

'Bird' by Anja Lau, aged eight ▷ years, from Westlodge Middle School.

Detail of 'Cliffside' in appliqué and straight stitches.

Landscape depicted in vertical and horizontal straight stitches. One area of seeding in the foreground shows another effect. (*Pat Morrish*.)

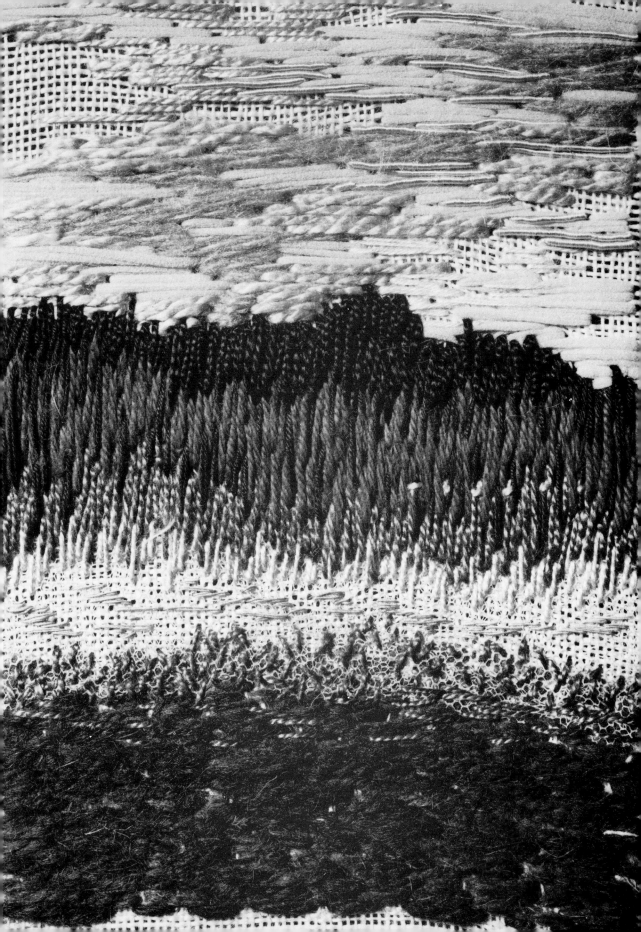

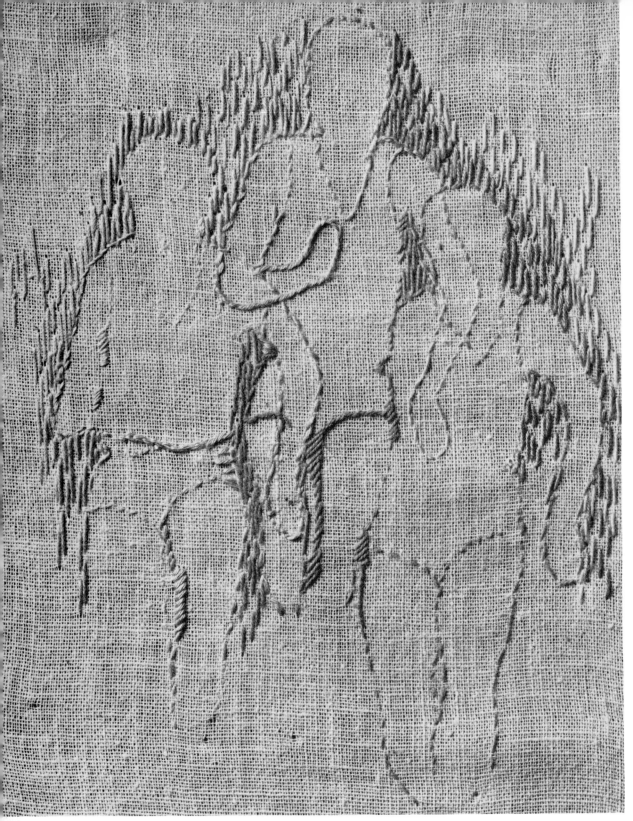

Straight stitches worked in the background spaces between the figures.
(*Ann Cunningham.*)

◁ A simple design inspired by tulip fields. Long, straight stitches worked on canvas and over plastic straws. (*June Linsley.*)

A simplified pattern inspired by the football crowd at Liverpool Cop. Scarves, rattles and figures partially depicted in straight stitches. (*Ann Sutton.*) ▽

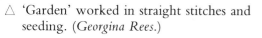

△ 'Garden' worked in straight stitches and seeding. (*Georgina Rees.*)

A simple still life depicted entirely in seeding and straight stitches. (*Phyllis Gunstone.*)

STRAIGHT STITCH – SATIN

A detail from a sleeve. The play of light on the direction of the satin stitches affects the tones, making the same colour lighter or darker. Chinese.

THORN STITCH

Even rows of thorn stitch worked in wool, cotton and textured yarns. (*Hilkka Dorey.*)

An interpretation of a garden scene worked in a wide range of threads. (*Jean Littlejohn.*)

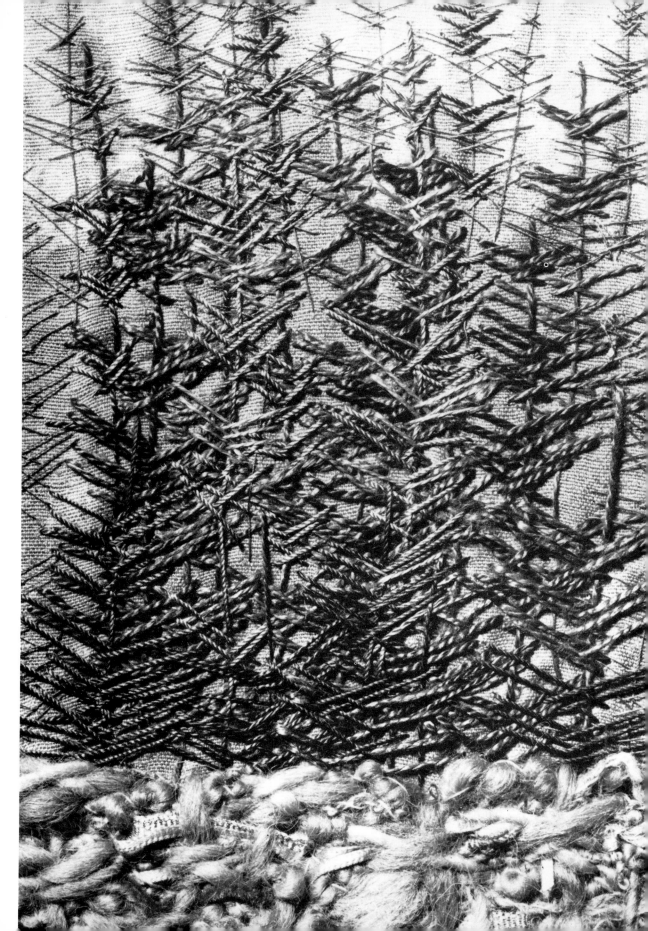

VELVET STITCH

Velvet stitch worked in wool, coton perlé, silk and strips of chamois leather, showing the loops at varying lengths, cut and uncut. (*Ann Sutton*.)

An interpretation of a section of hedgerow. The foreground is worked ▷ conventionally but with loops left uncut. The next section shows the stitch worked upside down and the ends couched in place. The top part is worked with random stitches: the loops have been wrapped, giving a tendril effect. (*Margaret Wilson*.)

WAVE STITCH

(Looped shading stitch)
First work vertical straight stitches.

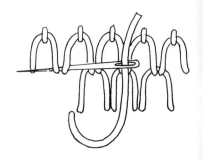

Wave stitch worked with even spacing but in a range of thick and thin threads which gives lacy and more solid effects.
(*Diana Spencer.*)

The initial straight stitches have been replaced by short bands of machined satin stitch with hand stitching worked into them, giving a most unusual effect. (*Diana Spencer*.)

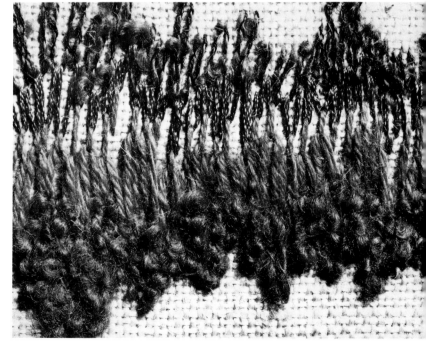

The stitch worked with irregular spacing in wool, weaving yarns and shiny rayon yarn. (*Diana Spencer*.)

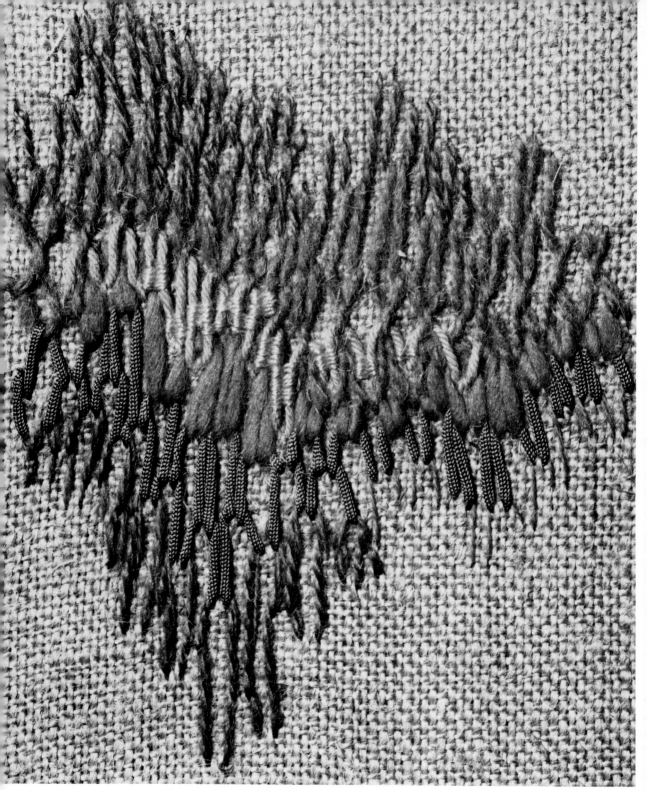

An uneven row of vertical stitches was first worked in the middle
section and wave stitches were then worked on the foundation stitches,
outwards in both directions. Needleweaving was worked over the
central threads; wool, perlé and a rayon macramé yarn.

WHEATEAR STITCH

Work two straight stitches at A and B. Bring the thread through below these stitches at C and pass the needle under the two straight stitches without entering the fabric. Insert the needle at C and bring it through at D.

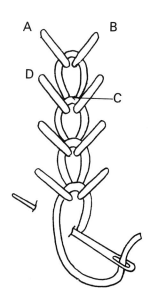

Lines of wheatear stitches worked in a variety of threads including plastraw, wool and fine ribbon. (*Pat Iles.*)

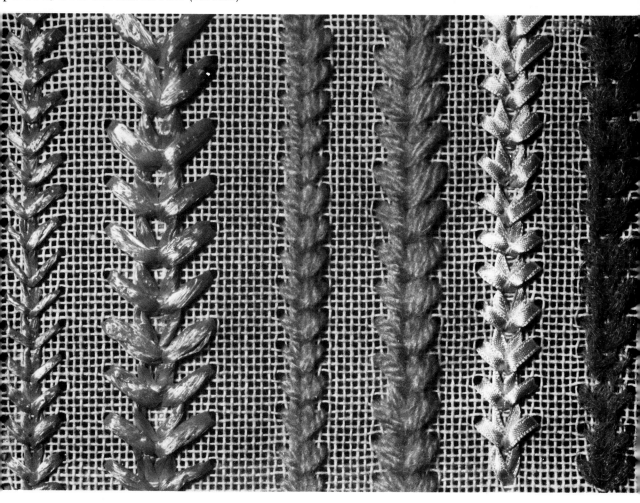

An attractive pattern made by working the stitch towards a centre
point. The emphasis has been placed on the loop with smaller straight
stitches. (*Pat Iles.*)

Large stitches worked with a small loop and long, loosely worked
straight stitches. Clusters of single wheatear stitches were worked first
and are just visible through the top stitching. (*Pat Iles.*)

An interesting sampler showing wheatear stitch worked as a filling stitch in the background; the straight stitches are worked almost horizontally. Parts of the top stitches have been wrapped with a shiny thread and show beads incorporated in the work process. (*Pat Iles.*)

WOVEN WHEELS
(Spider web filling stitch)

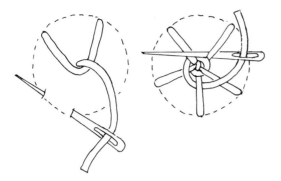

Varying-sized woven wheels worked closely together making an
unusual all-over texture. French knots have been worked between.
(*Maria Wetherall.*)

Ideas for design

The result, after working some stitches in a variety of ways, should be a collection of sample textures which may be constantly referred to – a stitch vocabulary. Many of these may be unusual and very unexpected. When worked in appropriate colours and scale these patches of stitchery might suggest undergrowth, grass, tiles, feathers, hair – the list is endless.

At this stage a personal approach to embroidery must come to the fore. It may be appropriate to work and express individual ideas in the following directions:

1 Stitched abstract textures
2 Formal abstract patterns
3 Stylized designs
4 Interpretative stitchery

The first style can be purely abstract and made up of layers or areas of stitchery, developing and stretching stitches to their limits. The challenge may be in planning and executing a piece of work so that the qualities of the thread and the patterns made by varying the stitch directions cast shadows or so that complex colour schemes feature. However, the colouring, texture and placing of the stitches might suggest a feeling, an atmosphere or an emotion. Strong, static, sombre-coloured areas of stitchery might suggest foreboding, despair or bleakness, while softly coloured, undulating shapes could show more sensitive, tender feelings. Long, bold diagonal stitches could give a vigorous feeling of movement, strength, forcefulness. Haphazard, strong, cross-hatched texture could hint at turmoil or chaos, whereas spiralling or circular shapes could represent continuity, an all-involving central theme or strength. The transmission of feelings or emotions is always a personal view and it is impossible to set rules and methods of interpretation.

Attempting to convey a feeling, an emotion or a thought process with stitches can make a good starting point for a design exercise.

The following headings may be helpful:

1 short, sharp stitches 'exploding' from a central area
2 long, bold diagonal stitches
3 short, sharp angles
4 gently rolling, undulating solid shapes
5 broken lines
6 circular, spiralling shapes
7 contours, repeating rhythms
8 random, isolated stitches
9 overlapping, enveloping

Having made the stitch patterns on the fabric, jot down notes indicating the emotions suggested by them.

Other starting points could be to work from words describing emotions. These can be jotted down. These emotions or feelings can be drawn from personal experience, literature or music. Descriptions of places, emotions, atmospheres or characters can often be the starting point for abstract stitched works.

Contemplate some of the following words and then interpret them by making pencil marks on paper or stitching into fabric:

ecstasy, crescendo
stillness, peacefulness, quiet, humour
disorder, chaos, puzzlement, questioning
warmth, coolness
menacing, tranquil, nervousness, hatred, joy
despair, harmony

Formal abstract patterns can be most exciting to look at and many foreign embroideries show simple devices of circular, square, striped and chevroned patterns most beautifully and skilfully executed. Turkish, Indian and some Greek Island embroidery illustrate this point.

When considering this style of working, achieving the balance between large and small shapes, line and mass, colours and

Detail from 'Colour Sound – Peace'. A great feeling of movement has been achieved by working the running stitches in this way. (*Julia Caprara*.)

contrasting texture within the design offers a continual challenge. A lavish, richly decorated area of raised stitches and metal threads could contrast with a simple area of linear stitches. The play of light on blocks of satin stitches arranged in different directions would give continually changing tonal effects.

Initially designing with simple cut paper shapes could be helpful, as well as pencil designs on graph paper and painted patterns. By contrasting solid areas and lacy ones, large and small pieces, thick and thin strips, interesting results can be obtained. Care should be taken to consider the background shapes, as

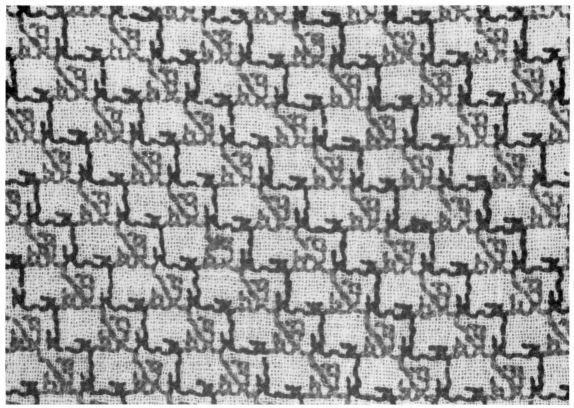

A simple pattern worked in double running stitch. From the Greek Islands. (*Embroiderers' Guild Collection.*)

motifs of the same shape and size can be boring. Once a pleasing pattern has evolved, stitches can be selected to build up the shapes on fabric.

Stylized designs come into the next category.

Figures, birds, trees and flowers are just some of many subjects that could be selected for a stylized design. Although, when interpreted, the subject can be recognizable, certain aspects of shape, colour and pattern are simplified or exaggerated. Little regard is given to perspective, proportion or a literal image. By selecting aspects of pattern or colour that particularly appeal from the design source, whether it be a bird, tree or other subject, these features can be enlarged or focused on in a number of eye-catching ways. Less appealing features can be understated or omitted altogether. No real attempt is made to suggest depth or other three-dimensional qualities.

Cut paper patterns can also be used for this style; often this approach disciplines the designer to see the shape simply whereas in making a pencil drawing the temptation is to represent the subject too closely.

A most effective surface made by working layers of raised chain band stitch. The straight threads between the chain on the first row of stitches were used as the foundation bars of the next and this procedure was repeated several times. The threads ranged from thick rug wool to soft embroidery and stranded cottons. (*Audrey King*.)

Section from a repeat pattern border: stylized birds worked in cross stitch. Central European.

The fourth approach is interpretative stitchery, which could be inspired by everyday scenes, objects or figures, and where there is an attempt to achieve, in part, the essential quality of an observed surface: an impression, not a literal, photographic style. Care should be taken to utilize the qualities of threads and stitches rather than using them to imitate the process of painting or drawing and becoming too illustrative.

A particular tonal quality, depth or form might be achieved by the closeness or openess of the stitchery, the tonal range of the colours and thickness of thread. The shape, growth, movement and characteristics of plants or shrubs in a garden scene could be simply depicted by the careful consideration of the placing and direction of the stitches.

The subject matter in this section is endless. It can include a more pictorial approach such as general views of people and places or the surface detail provided by a close–up lens, all of which can be real or imaginary. Possibly a detailed view of lichen on a roof or a section of rockface could provide a source for design, exploiting pleasing areas of colour and texture.

This last approach is really based on observation, learning to look and then selecting sections to interpret. A useful exercise is to take a paper frame and place it on varying parts of the general sketch, isolating particular features or areas of interest. Having found a section which includes an arrangement of shapes which appeal, this could then form the basis for an embroidered interpretation.

In conclusion, it is difficult to be emphatic about any of the mentioned design approaches as they depend on the individual's direction of study and particular interests. One or two of these ways of working could be considered and incorporated in one piece of work.

Design starting points:
1 Looking and sketching

The following section has been included to help readers find shapes and patterns that could be used and adapted into stitched surfaces. Before getting involved with large-scale designs it can be helpful to go out looking for unusual and interesting subjects. Ideas for embroidery can be more easily interpreted in stitchery if there is a reasonably clear aim or objective.

A selected number of subjects have been chosen with lists and appropriate questions. This approach can often be helpful for intensifying observation skills. By describing in words the characteristics of the various surfaces and shapes that are being observed, half of the creative decisions have been made. Accompanying these notes with simplified sketches will give greater clarity. Unusual or unexpected colour schemes, textural variations, patterns, grid networks, asymmetrical or symmetrical arrangements should be noticed and documented at all times.

Although the subjects listed are limited, the same type of questioning can apply to any subject − animals, birds, fish, machinery, transport, food or drinks etc.

OBSERVING: *buildings*

○ Are the buildings:

- large, tall, low, sprawling?
- made of brick, stone, wood or clad in pebble-dash or glass?

○ What shape are the:

- windows?
- doors, porches, canopies?
- chimney stacks and pots?

○ Are there any decorative features such as:

- ridge tiles, wrought-iron balconies?
- eaves, gargoyles?
- tile work or other patterned claddings?
- scaffolding, signs, lighting?

○ What material covers the roof:
- slate?
- pantiles?
- glass, thatch?
- corrugated materials?

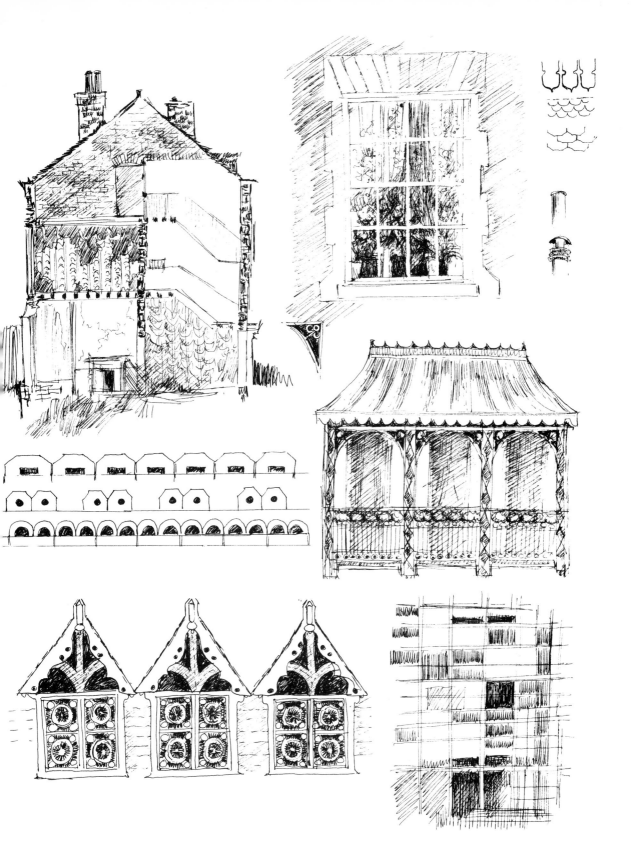

199

OBSERVING: *fences/walls*

○ Are they made of:

    – irregular-angled thin posts?
    – wooden slats and boards?
    – wire-mesh and concrete posts?
    – barbed wire?
    – wickerwork/wattle?

○ Does the wood contain:

    – subtle colour schemes?
    – varying-sized knots, holes, flaking bark?

○ Does the fence:

    – contain continuous line patterns?
    – cash shadows which form unusual pattern features?

○ How do the colours change:
    – when wet?
    – bathed in sunshine?
    – frosted or snow-covered?

○ Which feature or features could be exaggerated in the design process?

○ Are the walls made of brick, stone, flint, concrete blocks?

○ Are the brick walls eroding away, crumbling?

○ Are the bricks smooth, roughly textured, pitted?

○ Is there any natural growth such as lichen, moss, trailing plants, other vegetation?

○ Look at the range of colours and their proportions in individual stones or bricks.

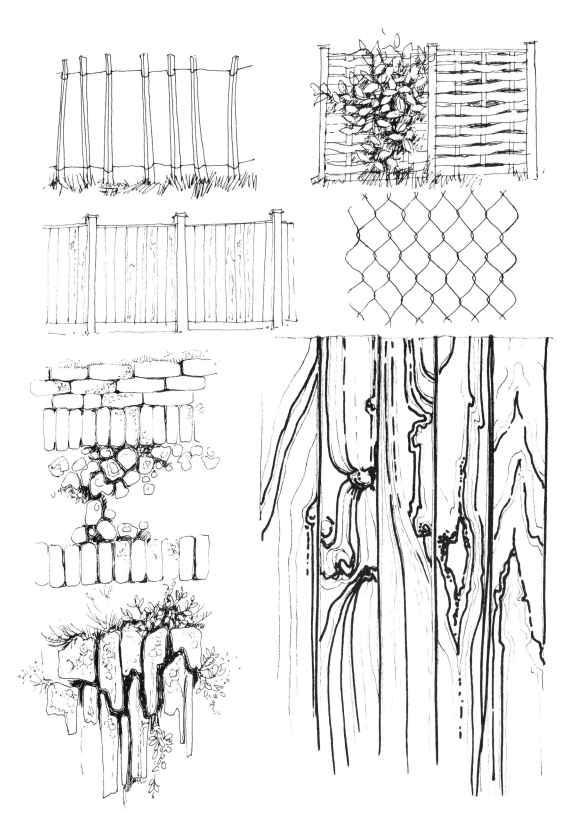

OBSERVING: *flowers*

○ Are the flowers:

- circular or in groups of circles?
- spiky, loopy?
- clustered, in rosettes?
- star-like?
- bell-shaped or drooping down?
- in massed dots?
- hanging like pendants?
- streaked, spotted, flecked, flushed?
- fringed, mottled or edged with other colours?
- growing in profusion or in isolated clumps?
- massed in areas or blocks of colour?
- like a kaleidoscope?
- slightly blurred and out of focus?
- banked, layered?
- creeping, trailing, climbing or intertwining?

○ Are the petals:

- waxy, leathery?
- like tissue paper?
- velvety?
- straw-like?

OBSERVING: *grasses*

○ Is the grass:

- growing upwards, abundantly, densely, sparsely or in tufts?
- coarse, fine, short or long?
- rough or smooth?
- green, grey/green, brown or tinged with pink, purple or any other colour?
- growing near water, sand pebbles?
- dull or shiny?
- fern-like or frond-like?
- broad-leaved?
- topped with bristles, spikelets, florets?
- nodding, swaying, quivering or very still?

○ Are the stems:

- delicate, slender, spreading, erect?
- ridged, jointed, flat, round or hairy?

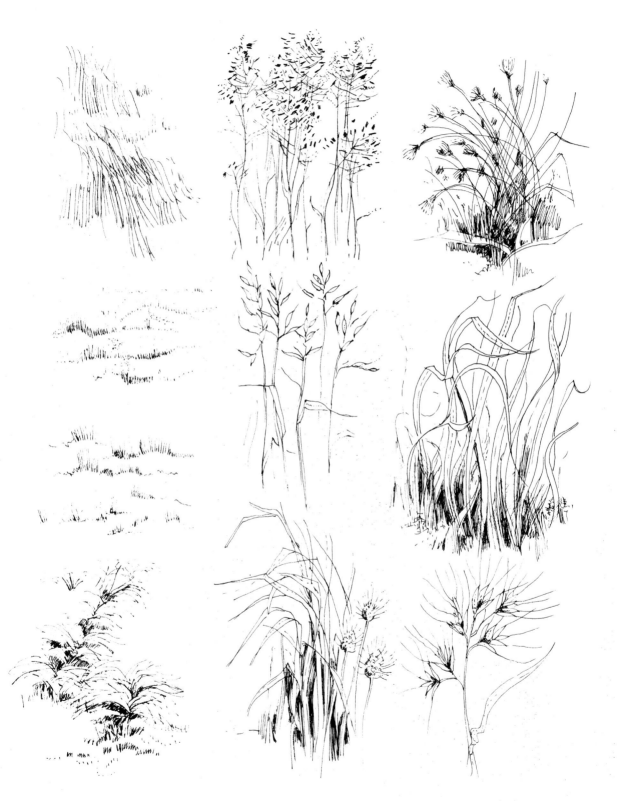

OBSERVING: *landscape/seascape*

○ Is the landscape:
- – undulating, contoured?
- – barren, bleak, menacing, overwhelming?
- – spiky, frilly?
- – open, spacious, airy?
- – craggy, rocky, mountainous?
- – patchworked, striped?

○ Is the sea:

- – still, quiet, smooth?
- – glittering, shiny, streaked?
- – pounding, crashing, rolling?
- – choppy, wavy, rippling?
- – swirling, splashing?
- – clear, muddy, cloudy, translucent?
- – grey, grey/green, khaki?
- – purple, seagreen, bottle green?
- – white, silver – or any other colour?

○ Are the figures:

– tall/thin, short/fat?
– standing erect, stooping, grouped together?
– in line, leaning, sitting, bending down?
– dressed in clothes which are multi-coloured, sombre?

○ Do the faces have features which could be exaggerated such as:

– moustaches, beards, side whiskers?
– shaggy eyebrows, deeply sunken eyes?
– deeply etched faces, bristles, make-up?

○ Is the hair:

– long, short, curly, straight, frizzy, in ringlets, plaited, crested, multi-coloured?

○ Is the hair, face or body adorned with jewellery, ribbons, glasses, hair-slides?

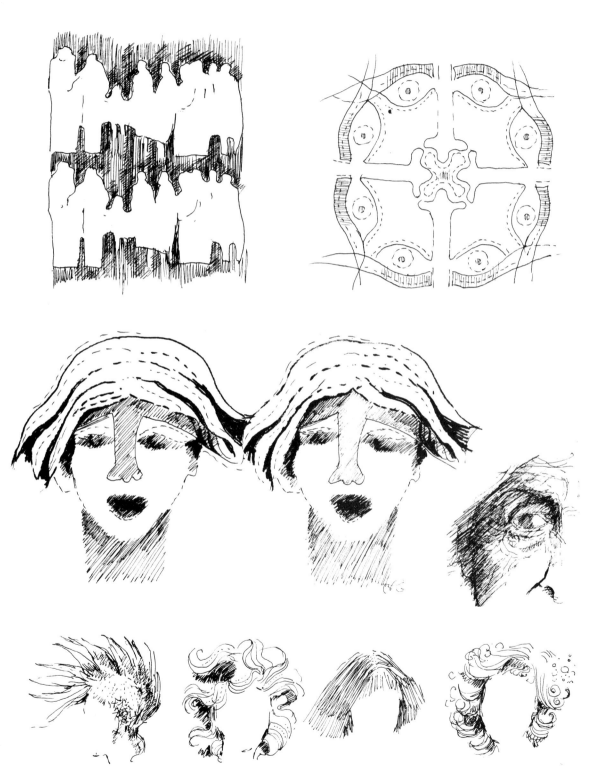

OBSERVING: *trees*

○ Are the trees:

    – growing closely together?
    – of the same type?
    – tall and thin?
    – broad and spreading?
    – small- or large-leafed, pollarded?

○ Which direction do the branches and twigs grow?

○ Do the leaves grow upwards, outwards or droop down?

○ Are the leaf shapes:

    – heart or kidney-shaped?
    – long, thin, serrated?
    – oval, smooth, hairy, prickly?
    – leathery, heavily veined or arranged in leaflets?

○ Is the bark:

    – fine grained and smooth?
    – ridged, flaky, patchy?
    – twisted in network patterns?
    – indented with long furrows?
    – cracked, fissured, scarred or covered in swellings, lumps or
      wartlike protrusions?

○ Are there any:

    – unusual or unexpected colour schemes?
    – parasites, fungi?

○ What shape, texture and colouring are the flowers, fruit, seeds?

Design starting points: 2 One-stitch pictures and patterns

As already experienced, there can be dozens of arrangements and surfaces made by the variations which can be achieved with just one stitch. Constance Howard has often said that she believes that one stitch can be worked in a multitude of ways and totally absorb and challenge a worker for a lifetime. This view is well illustrated by many respected artists who express their ideas in fabric and thread and use only a few stitches on any one piece of work.

As an exercise a stitch could be selected and a pattern or picture worked entirely in that stitch. A particular subject and style of design should be selected at the outset. It could be interpreted as a flat pattern: an arrangement of shapes where proportion, background spaces and colour combinations would be features to plan carefully. By contrast, in a more impressionistic piece, the tones and spacing of the stitches would need to be considered in depth. Earlier exercises featuring fine and coarse threads, closely spaced, contrasted by sparse, understated threadwork, could be a helpful reference. Layered stitches, bead-encrusted ones or those blocked in varying directions could also be inspiring. It should be remembered that a change of direction and scale can also totally transform the quality of one stitch.

'Trees' worked completely in straight stitches. Textured knitting wools, coton perlé and fine ribbons. (*Birthe Crawford.*)

A small picture inspired by euphorbia plants, worked mainly in detached chain stitch.

This charming picture was inspired by a sepia photograph of a family group. It is worked almost entirely in variations of detached buttonhole in fine threads. (*Barbara Hirst.*)

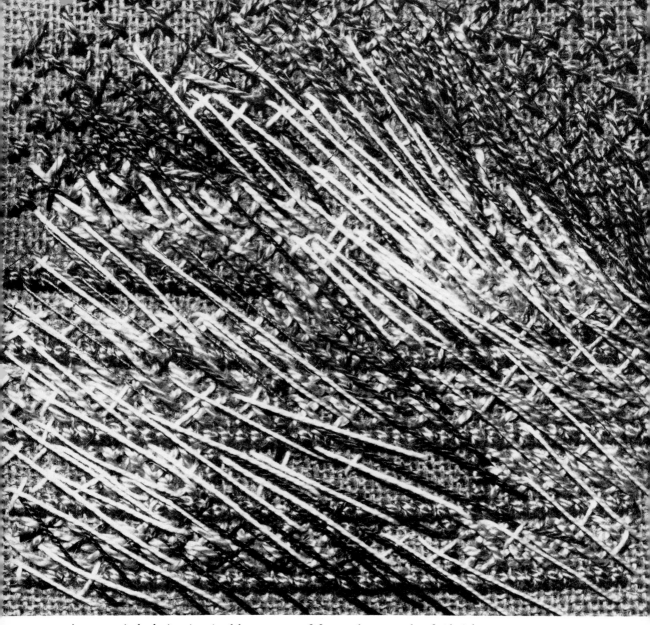

A cross stitch design inspired by an out-of-focus photograph of a brick wall. (*Janet Callender*.)

A small panel worked in close buttonhole stitch. Some areas have been worked in knotted buttonhole filling. (*Mary Bastow*.)

Detail from 'The Tree', worked entirely in straight stitches. (*Eirian Short.*)

Detail from 'The Moon', worked entirely in french knots and crewel wools. (*Eirian Short.*)

Detail from 'Life is Just a Little Bowl of Cherries'; some appliqué and straight stitches; long and short stitch, seeding. (*Audrey Walker*.)

◁ Layers of compost in a wire container interpreted in cross stitch worked in thick, thin, shiny and matt threads and fabric strips. (*Vicky Lugg*.)

Landscape interpreted in cretan stitch. (*Margaret Potts*.)

Design starting points:
3 Hand stitching with other techniques

Many embroiderers enjoy combining textile-related crafts, many of which can be enriched with the addition of hand stitching. Stitchery can change the quality of the surface and add another dimension to the work. It can also be a way to highlight particular areas of interest or the focal point.

Dyes feature more often these days in textile crafts. This is probably because of the fact that they are relatively cheap, readily available and can be used at home. Some dyes can be sprayed, sponged or brushed onto fabric to give a general impression of a design before certain areas are emphasized by stitching. Direct transfer dyes can be painted onto paper and the design then transferred by iron to the cloth. Pleasing effects can be obtained by tie and dye or batik and their unique patterned surfaces can also inspire the stitcher.

Knitting, crochet and weaving can all provide interesting ground fabrics to be stitched on. Many other embroidery techniques can incorporate surface stitchery: appliqué is one that comes to mind. The combination of hand and machine stitchery is a constant challenge and many artists continue to progress further in this area.

'The Secret Meeting.' Areas of dye were painted on calico and the surface enriched with haphazard blocks of straight stitches worked in fine silks. Inspired by a section viewed within a fragment of Welsh slate.

Simple flowers depicted in batik printing on cotton fabrics. The stems ▷ and other foliage have been worked in coral stitch in thick and thin threads. (*Sue Atkinson.*)

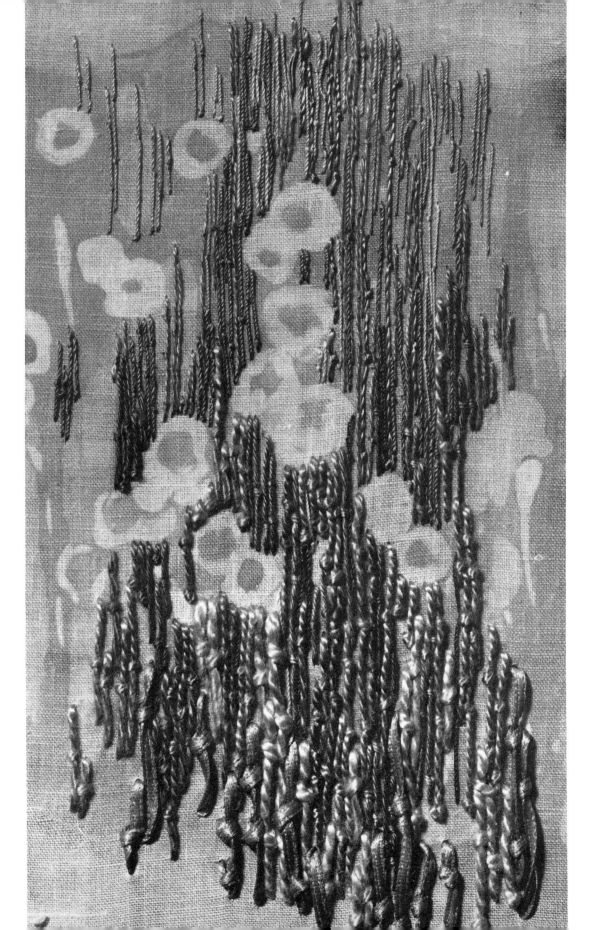

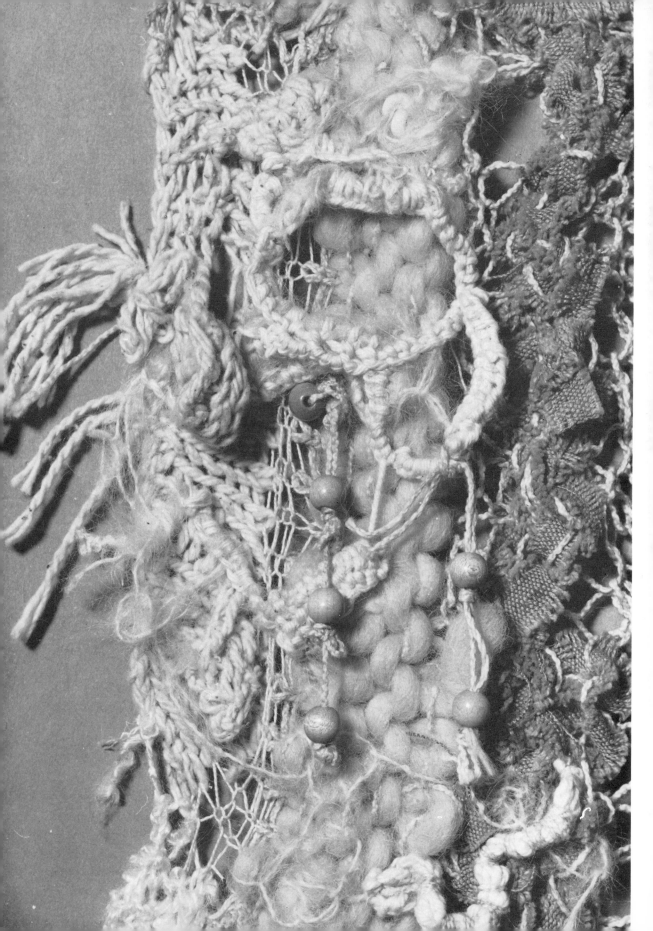

Detail from a large panel commemorating the work of John
Haslegrave OBE, commissioned by the City of Portsmouth. The house
is depicted in dye and machine embroidery which contrasts well with
the freer areas of hand stitchery: raised chain band, straight stitches and
seeding. (*Jean Littlejohn.*)

◁ Experimental knitting using several needle sizes; cotton threads, torn
strips of furnishing fabric and wool – areas of buttonhole stitch and
beads. (*Elaine Bonner.*)

Detail from 'A Rainbow Round my Shoulder' – appliqué, machine
embroidery and hand stitching. (*Audrey Walker*.)

Conclusion

Although some frustrations, difficulties and limitations may have been encountered with the stitch experiments, I hope that much joy, surprise and satisfaction has also been experienced.

When using stitch textures, always question whether the subject matter is suitable for interpretation in fabric and thread.

There is great enjoyment in using stitches for their own sake and allowing the properties of a certain stitch to limit and influence a way of working. However, by being fully acquainted with all aspects of a chosen stitch, the worker can eventually be in total control. Embroidery, and in particular stitchery, is quite unique and significantly different from any other medium. With experience and experimentation, embroiderers will create original stitched surfaces and be motivated to continue to develop and widen the boundaries of stitchery, expressing their individual ideas and feelings in the process.

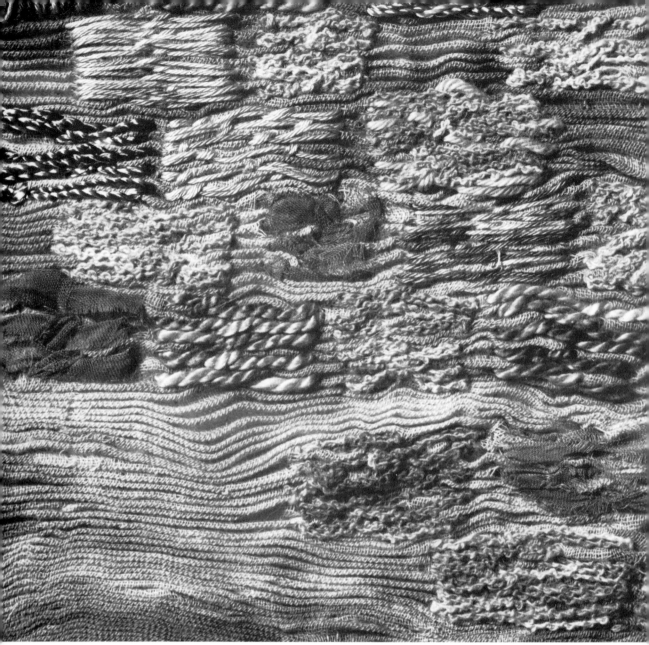

Smocking decorated with blocks of Bokhara couching in a variety of textured threads. (*Brenda Stockwell.*)

Books to read

STITCHES

Butler, Anne, *The Batsford Encyclopaedia of Embroidery Stitches*, Batsford 1979, paperback 1983

Butler, Anne, *Simple Stitches*, Batsford 1968

Christie, Mrs Archibald, *Samplers and Stitches*, Batsford 1920, paperback 1985

Howard, Constance, *The Constance Howard Book of Stitches*, Batsford 1979

Krevitsky, Nik, *Stitchery: Art and Craft*, Van Nostrand Reinhold 1966

100 Embroidery Stitches, J & P Coats Ltd 1967

Thomas, Mary, *Mary Thomas's Dictionary of Embroidery Stitches*, Hodder and Stoughton 1934

GENERAL DESIGN

Beaney, Jan, *Embroidery: New Approaches*, Pelham Books 1981

Beaney, Jan, *Buildings in Picture, Collage and Design*, Pelham Books 1976

Beaney, Jan, *Landscape in Picture, Collage and Design*, Pelham Books 1976

Beaney, Jan, *Textures and Surface Patterns*, Pelham Books 1978

The Embroiderers' Guild Practical Study Group, *Needlework School*, QED 1984

Howard, Constance, *Embroidery and Colour*, Batsford 1976

Howard, Constance, *Inspiration for Embroidery*, Batsford 1966, paperback 1985

Newland, Mary, and Walkland, Carol, *Printing and Embroidery*, Batsford 1977

Whyte, Kathleen, *Design in Embroidery*, Batsford 1983

Suppliers

UK

Borovick Fabrics Ltd
16 Berwick Street
London W1V 4HP

Angela Carr
The Old Rectory
Bruntingthorpe
Leicestershire LE17 5NR
(*Fabric transfer paints*)

Campden Weavers
16 Lower High Street
Chipping Campden
Gloucestershire GL55 6DY

Coats Domestic Marketing
  Division
39 Durham Street
Glasgow G41 1BS
(*Full range of Anchor embroidery
  threads, information and lists of
  stockists*)

de Denne Ltd
159/161 Kenton Road
Kenton
Harrow
Middlesex HA3 0EU

Dunlicraft Ltd
Pullman Road
Wigston
Leicester LE8 2DY
(*DMC threads, information and lists
  of stockists*)

John Lewis
Oxford Street
London W1

Mace & Nairn
89 Crane Street
Salisbury
Wiltshire SP1 2PY

MacCulloch and Wallis Ltd
25–26 Dering Street
London W1R 0BH

C.M. Offray and Son Ltd
Fir Tree Place
Church Road
Ashford
Middlesex TW15 2PH
(*Ribbons*)

Rowan Yarns
Rowan Dept E.M.
Green Lane Mill
Washpit
Holmfirth
West Yorkshire HD7 1RW
(*Chenille, tweeds, wool and cotton
  threads*)

The Weavers' Shop
Wilton Royal Carpet Factory
King Street
Wilton
Nr Salisbury
Wiltshire SP2 0AY
(*Thrums, long ends of unsorted
  yarns*)

Whaleys (Bradford) Ltd
Harris Court
Great Horton
Bradford
(*Good range of fabrics*)

A comprehensive and up-to-date
list of suppliers is printed in the
small ads section of *Embroidery*
magazine, published quarterly by
The Embroiderers' Guild,
Apartment 41, Hampton Court
Palace, East Molesey, Surrey
KT8 9AU and in *Crafts* magazine,
published every two months by
the Crafts Council, 8 Waterloo
Place, London SW1Y 4AT

USA

Casa de las Tejedoras
1619 East Edinger
Santa Ana
CA 92705

Contessa Yarns
Lebanon
CT 06249

Dharma Trading Company
1579 Solano Avenue
Berkeley
CA 947 04

Folklorico Yarn Company
436 University Avenue
Palo Alto
CA 94301

Heads or Tails
7977 Lake Street
River Forest
ILL 60305

Lily Mills
Elmore Corporation
PO Box 187
Spindale
NC 28160

The Needle's Point Studio
216 Apple Blossom Court
Vienna
VA 22180

The Pendleton Shop
PO Box 233
465 Jordan Road
Sedona
AZ 86336

The Rusty Needle
Gateway Centre
24000 Alicia Parkway
Mission Viejo
CA 92691

The Thread Shed
204 Fifth Avenue
Pittsburgh
PA 15222

CANADA

The Good Wool Shop
1103 Corydon Avenue
Winnipeg R3M OX3

Handicraft Wools Ltd
Box 378
Streetsville
Ontario L5M 2B9

Mile End Store
83000 SE McLoughlin Blvd
Portland
Ontario

The Village Weaver
551 Church Street
Toronto
Ontario M47 2EZ

Index to stitches

Stitch names in capital letters have principal entries in the stitches sections of the book (pages 27–188)